Writing to Learn
THE ESSAY

Writing to Learn
THE ESSAY

LOU J. SPAVENTA
MARILYNN L. SPAVENTA

Santa Barbara City College

Boston   Burr Ridge, IL   Dubuque, IA   Madison, WI   New York   San Francisco   St. Louis
Bangkok   Bogotá   Caracas   Lisbon   London   Madrid
Mexico City   Milan   New Delhi   Seoul   Singapore   Sydney   Taipei   Toronto

McGraw-Hill Higher Education

A Division of The **McGraw-Hill** *Companies*

WRITING TO LEARN: THE ESSAY

Published by McGraw-Hill, an imprint of The McGraw-Hill Companies, Inc., 1221 Avenue of the Americas, New York, NY 10020.

 This book is printed on recycled, acid-free paper containing 10% postconsumer waste.

2 3 4 5 6 7 8 9 0 QPD/QPD 0 9 8 7 6 5 4 3 2

ISBN 0–07–230756–0

Vice president and editor-in-chief: *Thalia Dorwick*
Editorial director: *Tina B. Carver*
Director of marketing: *Tom Dare*
Developmental editor: *Robert Hemmer*
Senior project manager: *Peggy J. Selle*
Production supervisor: *Sandy Ludovissy*
Coordinator of freelance design: *David W. Hash*
Cover/text designer: *Juan Vargas*
Cover illustration: *©PhotoDisc Inc., 1999*
Supplement coordinator: *Sandra M. Schnee*
Compositor: *David Corona Design*
Typeface: *11/13 Stone Sans*
Printer: *Quebecor Printing Book Group/Dubuque, IA*

The credits section for this book begins on page 172 and is considered an extension of the copyright page.

Library of Congress Cataloging-in-Publication Data

Spaventa, Louis J.
   Writing to learn / Louis J. Spaventa, Marilynn L. Spaventa. — 1st ed.
      p.   cm.
   Includes indexes.
   Contents: [bk. 1] The sentence — bk. 2. The paragraph — bk. 3. From paragraph to essay — bk. 4. The essay.
ISBN 0–07–230753–6 (bk.1) — ISBN 0–07–230754–4 (bk. 2) — ISBN 0–07–230755–2 (bk. 3) — ISBN 0–07–230756–0 (bk. 4)
1. English language—Textbooks for foreign speakers.   2. English language—Rhetoric—Problems, exercises, etc.   3. Report writing—Problems, exercises, etc.   I. Spaventa, Marilynn.   II. Title.

PE1128 .S697   2001
808'.042—dc21   99–057820
                                                            CIP

www.mhhe.com

CONTENTS

Unit 2: Family and Relationships   28

Unit 3: Education   56

Unit 4: Work 82

PREFACE

To the Instructor

WRITING TO LEARN is a four-book ESL writing series aimed at adult learners of English from diverse educational backgrounds. The series focuses both on the process of writing and on writing as a product. The goal of the series is to help students learn how to write for academic and vocational success. Each book in the series makes use of student skills and experience to generate writing topics while providing guided practice of appropriate vocabulary and grammar, English writing conventions, writing, editing, rewriting, and journal writing. Each chapter of books 1 and 2 and each unit of book 3 in the series begins with a visual image that leads to discussion and writing. The fourth text uses readings as prewriting prompts. WRITING TO LEARN begins with an elementary text designed to improve student ability to write accurate and descriptive English sentences. The upper elementary to intermediate level text focuses on writing paragraphs. The third or intermediate level text takes the student from paragraph writing to organizing, writing, and editing essays. The final book at the advanced level concentrates on improving student essay writing skills and enhancing essay writing style.

Each book in the series is divided into six units. Books 1 and 2, *The Sentence* and *The Paragraph,* have two chapters in each unit while books 3 and 4, *From Paragraph to Essay* and *The Essay,* have just six units each. The reason for the difference is to create more and shorter lessons for the elementary to lower intermediate levels, and fewer but longer more challenging lessons at the intermediate to advanced levels of writing.

Here are the unit themes:

Unit One: Myself and Others

Unit Two: Family and Relationships

Unit Three: Education

Unit Four: Work

Unit Five: Leisure and Recreation

Unit Six: The Natural World

Students who work through several texts in the series will have the opportunity to explore the same theme from different perspectives.

The use of icons to indicate pair and group work is meant to facilitate classroom organization while eliminating repetitive instructions—the number indicates the total number of students needed to form the group. You will also notice that exercises use names of students from a variety of cultures, because we recognize that students will use English to communicate with others from diverse ethnic and linguistic groups. Finally, be sure to follow each unit in the Instructor's Edition for helpful suggestions and instructions for activities that are not included in the student text.

Organization

Each unit is divided into the following four sections:

A. Prewriting   In *The Essay*, each unit begins with prewriting activities based on a photograph and a reading. Prewriting activities include vocabulary learning, pair work, group work, and discussion. It is important for students to understand writing as a process that begins with creative reflection and communication.

B. Structure   Grammar activities include review of English grammar verb tenses and practice in writing accurate and varied sentences. Readings in the Structure section continue to develop the theme of the unit. Although the Structure section introduces grammar with example, explanation, and practice exercises, *The Essay* is not meant to be a grammar text. Grammar has been incorporated as a tool for expressing one's thoughts in more sophisticated sentence structure rather than as an end in itself.

C. Writing and Editing   Activities in this section are devoted to improving writing skills, especially employing the vocabulary and grammar practiced in sections A and B. A third reading provides more vocabulary and additional perspective on the theme of the unit. You will notice that we have not included sample student paragraphs and essays for students to follow in the writing section. In many texts, writing samples are provided with the expectation that students will diligently work with the sample to produce their own personalized writing. In fact, this rarely happens and students are more likely to be constricted by the model. In this series, the writing models appear in the Structure and Editing sections to encourage students to alter the samples and make the language their own. Each unit requires an extensive writing and revising assignment that demands at least two drafts and a peer editing phase. You can have students keep these assignments in a folder to develop a portfolio.

D. Journal Assignment   The personal, unedited, daily writing practice that journal writing affords is an important part of the process of writing well, especially for students writing in English as a Second Language. There is a variety of journal writing assignments at the end of each unit in this book. These assignments allow students to synthesize and expand upon what they are studying in each unit.

You will need to clarify for your students how often you expect them to write and how much writing they should produce. You will also need to decide how you will respond to student journal writing.

Here are a few suggestions.

- Respond only to the content of what is written in the journal.

- Look for positive examples of vocabulary and grammar usage consistent with each unit and highlight or underline them in student journals.

- Tell students you are going to read their journals with an eye toward a particular kind of writing: a descriptive sentence, an opinion, a comparison, an analysis or explanation, and so on. Then identify that writing when you come across it in student journals.

- Ask students to read something from their journals during class time. Ask the students listening to respond in writing to what they hear.

- Each week, read selected journal entries aloud to the entire class to inspire and foster respect among students of each other as writers.

Appendices   Each text contains appendices of grammar and writing conventions for student reference. During your first class meeting, when you familiarize students with the book, make sure you take some time to point out the appendices and what they contain. Students too often discover appendices at the end of a course.

Instructor's Edition   The Instructor's Edition of *The Essay* contains unit-by-unit notes of explanation, advice, suggestions, and reproducible structure quizzes for each unit. Each unit has a suggestion for a video clip that compliments the readings and the theme of the unit. An icon ✎ is used to indicate a note for the instructor.

Web Site   The *Writing to Learn* web site can be located through the McGraw-Hill, Inc. web site at <www.mhhe.com> This interactive site should be useful to instructors and students. For instructors, the site can be a virtual teacher's room, where instructors can raise questions and exchange ideas and activities related to this series. Students can post and read writing assignments for each unit and thus expand the walls of their classroom.

The Essay

This fourth book in the series emphasizes writing well-organized, interesting essays with varied sentence structure. A variety of readings are used to expand vocabulary, encourage discussion, and foster greater expression of opinion. Although topics cover both vocational and academic issues, writing assignments in this text are academic in nature. Student success in using this book should be based on ability to create a meaningful essay from the beginning step of brainstorming information to redrafting for style, grammaticality, effect on the reader, and content. So while one goal of the text is to expose students to the form of the English essay, another goal is to give them some tools to use in creating their own essays.

Each unit contains at least three readings on the unit topic. The structure exercises follow the context of the reading. Student essays, excerpts from novels and nonfiction texts, as well as magazine and newspaper articles provide a variety of perspectives and styles. Readings were selected because of their content, variety of style, and clear, interesting writing. They are not all models of the "five paragraph" academic essay, because not all good writing follows that format. Although we feel students of English as a Second Language should learn the five paragraph model, it is important for us to acknowledge that it is not the only model.

The First Lesson

Begin your first class with an exercise that helps your students become familiar with this text. You can do this orally, in writing, or both. Students should work in pairs or small groups. Students have their first task on page xv. A familiarization exercise is contained in the **To the Student** part of the introduction to *The Essay*.

Question your students about the names of the six units, the number of sections in each unit, the number and names of the appendices, and their thoughts about the use of each unit section and appendix.

Acknowledgments

First and foremost, we acknowledge the debt of thanks we owe to our students at Santa Barbara City College, whose interests and concerns were the catalyst that led us to embark on this writing project. We also would like to thank our colleagues at City College, especially Frank Lazorchik and Bophany Huot, as well as others in the larger field of ESOL writing who often made valuable suggestions to us about our manuscript.

This book and this series would not have been written without the encouragement and persistence of Tim Stookesberry, Aurora Martínez, and Pam Tiberia at McGraw-Hill, and our series editor—the inimitable, indefatigable, and empathetic Bob Hemmer.

Should you have any suggestions or comments, we would be happy to receive them from you in writing, via email, or at our web site. You can write to us in care of the ESL Department, Santa Barbara City College, Santa Barbara, California, 93109, USA. Our email address is spaventa@sbcc.net.

Lou and Marilynn Spaventa
Santa Barbara, California

To the Student

Welcome to *The Essay!*

The goal of this book is to help you write well in English and to learn how to organize your ideas in an essay form that you will need as you continue your studies in a North American academic institution.

This text uses the process approach to writing. This means that to produce a good product, there is first a process to follow. You may already have experience with this approach from previous writing courses. Work with a partner and see if you can order the following steps of the process approach.

a. first draft   1) _____

b. brainstorming a writing topic   2) _____

c. revising and editing for a second draft   3) _____

d. narrowing down a topic   4) _____

e. organizing the information   5) _____

f. read and discuss the topic   6) _____

Before using this, or any text, it is useful to explore the organization of the book.

This book has six units. Each unit has a topic that you will discuss and write about. Topics vary from personal to scientific. The topic for Unit One is Myself and Others. Look for the topics of the other units in the Table of Contents. Write the names of the topics below.

Unit One   Myself and Others_____

Unit Two   _____

Unit Three   _____

Unit Four   _____

Unit Five   _____

Unit Six   _____

Which topic do you think will be most interesting for you? Put a star next to that topic.

Take five minutes to skim through the units. Look only at the first page or two of each unit. Then return to this page and write down whatever words or thoughts come into your mind.

_____

_____

_____

Each unit has four sections. Match the section with its description. Draw a line from the section to its description.

Section	Description
Prewriting	practices English grammar
Structure	gives ideas for writing on your own, offers help with organization or grammar
Writing and Editing	prepares you for writing by reading on the topic, learning vocabulary, and offering ideas to discuss with classmates
Journal Assignment	has exercises to improve your essay writing skills

Look for these icons in the text . These icons indicate that the exercise can best be done with a partner or group. An important part of the writing process is articulating your thoughts to others orally, before writing.

Your instructor will decide how to use this book in the best way for you. We designed *The Essay* as a workbook, so please write in it. We hope you enjoy working with the book. Remember that learning to write well is a skill, which like any other skill requires practice and reflection. Write a lot about what you feel and think to become a confident writer. Learn a lot!

Lou and Marilynn Spaventa

Writing to Learn
THE ESSAY

Myself and Others

A Prewriting

Exercise 1. Meeting your classmates   Our spontaneous thoughts and our recent experiences can tell another person a lot about us. Write three sentences about how you are feeling now beginning with *I*.

> **EXAMPLE:** I am feeling a little nervous about this writing class.

1. _____

2. _____

3. _____

Now write three sentences about yourself using *my*. This time write something about people who are close to you or things that are important to you.

> **EXAMPLE:** My brother studied English at this school two years ago.

4. _____

5. _____

6. _____

We are often the object of other people's words and actions. Write three sentences about yourself using *me* that tell what someone has said or done to you recently.

> **EXAMPLE:** A strange woman asked me for money while I was waiting for the bus.

7. _____

8. _____

9. _____

 Exchange books with a partner. Read each other's sentences. Circle at least four sentences that you would like to know more about. Return each other's books. Then read what your partner has circled. Talk about at least two of those sentences, giving more detail.

 Exercise 2. Like me list   Use the list of question prompts that follow to find out who is like you. Those who are not like you are different, so only write down the names of those like you for this exercise. Walk around the room and ask people questions. Do not ask the same person more than one question.

> **EXAMPLE:** special about . . . hometown
>
> What's special about your hometown?

Prompts

1. special about . . . hometown _____

2. difficult about . . . language . . . speak _____

3. close to . . . in . . . family _____

4. why . . . studying _____

5. when . . . start studying . . . English _____

6. biggest problem with English _____

7. what are . . . plans . . . the future _____

8. do in free time _____

9. makes you happy _____

10. frustrates you _____

Now tell your group who is like you. For example, tell your group who comes from the same place you do and who speaks your language.

Exercise 3. Peak experiences When things happen to us that are unforgettable, we use words like *the best, the worst, the most,* and *the least.* With your partner, read over the following phrases and ask each other questions.

EXAMPLE: movie seen

What's the worst movie you've ever seen?

What's the most romantic movie you've ever seen?

the best	day
the worst	gift
the most (adj.)	thing done
the least (adj.)	thing learned
	game attended
	experience
	concert been to
	fear
	advice received
	wish
	accomplishment

Exercise 4. "Cooking with Mattie" Read this excerpt from an award-winning high school English essay.

From "Cooking With Mattie"
by Cara Baker

I poked my head into the kitchen and whispered, "Hellooo." That's my code to let Mattie know I'm hungry.

"I see you, little C. B. I'm making your favorite dinner right now." Chicken parmigiana and mashed potatoes (I know it sounds like a disgusting pair, but not when Mattie makes it).

"And no one makes it like you, Mattie. I've had a lot of chicken parmigiana, and no one has ever come close to yours, never mind top it."

"Haaa! That's why I like making it for you, little C. B. I always love compliments."

Mattie is the mother of my best friend, Charlie. Mattie is a diminutive African-American woman with curly black hair that just tickles her ears and a sparkling smile that she wears frequently. Fittingly, she calls me her other daughter, her paler daughter—the one who didn't get any sun.

Mattie's the best listener I've ever met and she is always genuinely concerned with what I have to say. A year ago Charlie and I were handed a dilemma. A friend wrote a poem to us expressing his wish "to end it all." We didn't know if he would kill himself or if he was just calling out for help. I phoned Mattie.

I won't pretend that I remember every line of that conversation, but what I do recall is that not once did she tell me what to do. Mattie guided me to the right decision by telling me to ask myself what would help my friend the most. She revealed that I knew what was right all along.

Mattie is more like family to me than anyone except my mom. She's not only watched me grow, she's played a large part in my growth. She is truly a chef. She's not only added some of the ingredients to my soul that help make me who I am, she's been one of the ingredients herself.

Write synonyms from the reading for the underlined words that follow and then write an original sentence demonstrating your comprehension of the word.

New vocabulary

1. *I <u>put</u> my head into the kitchen.*

   SYNONYMS: _____

   SENTENCE: _____

2. *That's my <u>secret symbol</u> to let Mattie know I'm hungry.*

   SYNONYMS: _____

   SENTENCE: _____

3. *. . . with curly black hair that just <u>lightly touches</u> her ears . . .*

   SYNONYMS: _____

   SENTENCE: _____

4. *<u>Appropriately</u>, she calls me her other daughter . . .*

   SYNONYMS: _____

   SENTENCE: _____

5. *. . . she is always <u>truly</u> concerned with what I have to say.*

   SYNONYMS: _____

   SENTENCE: _____

6. *She <u>showed</u> that I knew what was right all along.*

   SYNONYMS: _____

   SENTENCE: _____

Writing to Learn: *The Essay*

Exercise 5. Mattie and C. B. You now know part of a story that tells of Mattie and C. B.'s relationship. What more would you like to know about them? In the space provided, write three questions to each person.

To Mattie

1. _____

_____

2. _____

_____

3. _____

_____

To C. B.

1. _____

_____

2. _____

_____

3. _____

_____

 Pretend that you are Mattie and that your partner is C. B. Ask your partner the questions you wrote to C. B. Your partner will ask you the questions to Mattie. Then change roles. Make sure to write down the answers to each question.

 Join with another pair and read your questions and answers. Do you notice any similarities in the questions that the four of you have written to Mattie and C. B.?

Exercise 6. What makes a person good?   In the story, C. B. feels very warm towards Mattie. She feels Mattie is like a mother to her. Why does she feel this way? What makes Mattie a good person in C. B.'s eyes? Write your answer in the space provided.

Now think about a good person that you know. Think about the good qualities of that person. For each quality, give an example. A friend of one of the authors of this book is given as one example here.

EXAMPLE: *Person*—Cliff

Quality—loyalty

Example—I know that I can count on him to be a good friend even though we live far away from each other, and we only see each other once a year.

Now write down the name of the good person you know. Write down two or three qualities and examples of the quality.

Person _____

Quality _____

Example _____

_____

_____

In your group, talk about the good person you know. Allow the other people in the group to ask you questions about that person.

B Structure

> ## Good Descriptions
>
> In this Structure session, you are going to concentrate on building good description into your writing. The three structures you will work on are adjective clauses*, reduced adjective clauses, and prepositional phrases. Here is an example of each type.
>
> **Adjective clause**
>
> Mattie, *who was a good cook*, had prepared C. B.'s favorite dish.
>   *adjective clause*
>
> An adjective clause describes a noun. An adjective clause follows the noun and begins with the relative pronouns *who, which, that, whose, when, where,* or *why.*
>
> **Reduced adjective clause**
>
> C. B., *fidgeting with her hair*, was nervous as she talked to Mattie.
>   *reduced adjective clause*
>
> A reduced adjective clause describes a noun. A reduced adjective clause follows the noun. The relative pronoun and the *be* form of the verb are deleted.
>
> **Prepositional phrase**
>
> Mattie was a small woman *with black curly hair.*
>   *prepositional phrase*
>
> A prepositional phrase consists of a preposition and noun or adjective and noun. There is no verb in a prepositional phrase.
>
> * Adjective clauses are also called relative clauses.

Exercise 1. Recognizing adjective clauses, reduced adjective clauses, and prepositional phrases   First, underline the adjective clause, reduced adjective clause, or prepositional phrase in each sentence. Then rewrite the sentence as two separate sentences.

> **EXAMPLE:** C. B. was a young girl <u>who was very close to her best friend's mother</u>.
>   *adjective clause*
>
> **REWRITE:** C. B. was a young girl. She was very close to her best friend's mother.

1. Mattie was a woman who could really cook well.

_____

2. Charlie, whose best friend was C. B., was Mattie's daughter.

_____

3. C. B. is a person with a really big appetite for home cooking.

_____

4. Mattie, preparing chicken parmigiana in her kitchen, was happy to see C. B. walk in.

_____

5. Charlie and C. B. were sisters of different skin colors.

_____

6. The dish that C. B. liked to eat was chicken parmigiana and mashed potatoes.

_____

7. Poking her head into the kitchen, C. B. saw Mattie.

_____

8. Mattie, busy with preparing C. B.'s favorite food, was not too busy to chat with her.

_____

9. C. B. often asked Mattie, whose reputation as a wise person was well known.

_____

10. The kitchen is a place where families often have serious talks.

_____

11. With her wisdom, warmth, and patience, Mattie taught C. B. a lot about life.

_____

12. Mattie prepared chicken parmigiana, which is an Italian dish.

_____

Exercise 2. "Living in Tongues" Read this excerpt from an autobiographical article by a multilingual person.

From "Living in Tongues"
by Luc Sante

The first thing you have to understand about my childhood is that it mostly took place in another language. I was raised speaking French, and did not begin learning English until I was nearly 7 years old. Even after that, French continued to be the language I spoke at home with my parents. (I still speak only French with them to this day.) This fact inevitably affects my recall and evocation of my childhood, since I am writing and primarily thinking in English. There are states of mind, even people and events, that seem inaccessible in English, since they are defined by the character of the language through which I perceived them. My second language has turned out to be my principal tool, my means for making a living, and it lies close to the core of my self-definition. My first language, however, is coiled underneath, governing a more primal realm.

French is a pipeline to my infant self, to its unguarded emotions and even to its preserved sensory impressions. I can, for example, use language as a measure of pain. If I stub my toe, I may profanely exclaim, in English, "Jesus!" But in agony, like when I am passing a kidney stone, I become uncharacteristically reverent, which is only possible for me in French. *"Petit Jésus!"* I will cry, in the tones of nursery religion. When I babble in the delirium of a fever or talk aloud in my sleep, I have been told by others, I do so in French.

List new vocabulary below. Write an original sentence for each word, demonstrating your comprehension of the word.

```
┌─────────────────────────────────────────────────────────────┐
│                      New vocabulary                           │
│                                                               │
│                                                               │
│                                                               │
│                                                               │
│                                                               │
│                                                               │
│                                                               │
│                                                               │
│                                                               │
│                                                               │
│                                                               │
│                                                               │
│                                                               │
│                                                               │
└─────────────────────────────────────────────────────────────┘
```

Exercise 3. Combining sentences with adjective clauses   Combine each pair of sentences about Luc Sante.

EXAMPLE: Luc Sante speaks English. Luc Sante grew up speaking French.

Luc Sante, *who speaks English,* grew up speaking French.

1. Luc spoke French as a child. He mostly speaks English now.

_____

2. He has an emotional attachment to French. French is his first language.

_____

3. Luc earns his living as an artist. He lives in New Jersey.

_____

4. Sante remembers the language of his childhood. (A time) He spoke French with his parents.

_____

5. Luc curses even better in French. He curses in English.

_____

6. French is deeply part of Sante. French is the language of his soul.

_____

7. Sante's parents live in the United States. The United States is an English-speaking country.

_____

8. Sante spent his early childhood in another country. People spoke French in that country.

_____

9. Bilinguals are interesting people. Their feet are in two worlds.

_____

10. Sante's bilingualism makes him a richer person. Sante has insight into two cultures.

_____

Take turns reading sentences 1 through 10. If there are big differences in how you each completed a sentence, discuss whether the differences are okay. If you are not sure about the grammar, make a note. When you have finished the exercise, ask your instructor for help.

Exercise 4. Building adjective clauses   Following is a list of words that are used as relative pronouns in adjective clauses.

Relative Pronouns in Adjective Clauses

For subject of a clause	*who which that*
For object of a clause	*who (whom)* which that*
For possessive	*whose*
For place	*where*
For reason	*why*
For time	*when*
Combined with preposition	*to whom to which to whose to where*

* Whom is gradually being replaced by who in conversational English. However, whom is the written object relative pronoun form.

Decide which word in the pair of sentences needs to be replaced by a relative pronoun. Then combine the pair of sentences using a relative pronoun.

> **EXAMPLE:** C. B. is a young woman. C. B. likes to eat chicken parmigiana. *(C. B. occurs twice and needs to be replaced by a subject relative pronoun.)*
>
> *C. B. is a young woman who likes to eat chicken parmigiana.*

1. Mattie loves to create fancy dishes. Mattie cooks on a huge old gas stove.

   _____

2. Luc learned English in school. Luc's parents taught him French at home.

   _____

3. Mattie is a diminutive African-American woman. C. B. loves Mattie.

   _____

4. Luc cries out in French at times. At times he is in great pain.

   _____

5. Mattie spends a lot of time in the kitchen. Mattie cooks in the kitchen.

   _____

6. New Jersey is the state. Luc lives in New Jersey.

   _____

Exercise 5. Writing adjective clauses about yourself Think about yourself. Think about how you spend your day, whom you see, what you do, how you feel about the things you do, what you want each day. Now write one sentence about your life using *who*.

> **EXAMPLE:** I am a person who likes to read.

1. _____

Write one sentence about your life using *that*.

> **EXAMPLE:** I like the shirt that I bought yesterday.

2. _____

Write one sentence about your life using *whose.*

    EXAMPLE: The professor whose course I took last term is now my friend.

3. _____

Write one sentence about places you go using *where.*

    EXAMPLE: I go to a local bookstore where I can find any book I want.

4. _____

Write one sentence about a time you do a certain thing using *when.*

    EXAMPLE: Final exam time is a time when I always feel nervous.

5. _____

Exercise 6. Reducing adjective clauses When an adjective clause using *who, which,* or *that* is about the subject, the clause can be reduced to an adjective phrase.

    EXAMPLE 1: The woman who is cooking the meal is my mother.
    The woman <u>cooking the meal</u> is my mother.
        adjective phrase

    EXAMPLE 2: C. B. is a person who is loyal to her friends.
    C. B. is a person <u>loyal to her friends</u>.
        adjective phrase

    EXAMPLE 3: The dishes that are on the table are chipped.
    The dishes <u>on the table</u> are chipped.
        adjective phrase
        (prepositional phrase
        modifying a noun)

Reduce these sentences with adjective clauses to sentences with adjective phrases in them.

1. C. B. is the one who is talking to Mattie.

_____

2. Luc is the person that is sitting in that chair.

_____

3. The dog that is barking at the mailman is still a puppy.

_____

4. Mattie has a recipe book that contains hundreds of recipes.

_____

5. Luc's parents, who are fluent in French, don't speak English well.

_____

6. The car that is in front of our house belongs to Luc.

_____

7. The language that is being spoken is Italian.

_____

8. The cat, which is on the window sill, is named Sam.

_____

C Writing and Editing

Exercise 1. Time line for an autobiography Read over the time line below. Make notes for each period in your life.

Time line for the first part of life

| early childhood | elementary school days | teenage years | young adulthood |

Notes:

1. early childhood _____

2. elementary school days _____

3. teenage years _____

4. young adulthood _____

Writing to Learn: *The Essay*

Exercise 2. "This Is Me"   Read these excerpts from the life of the famous U.S. psychologist, Carl Rogers.

From "This Is Me"
by Carl Rogers

My Early Years

(1)   I was brought up in a home marked by close family ties, a very strict and uncompromising religious and ethical atmosphere, and what amounted to a worship of the virtue of hard work. I came along as the fourth of six children. My parents cared a great deal for us, and had our welfare almost constantly in mind. They were also, in many subtle and affectionate ways, very controlling of our behavior. It was assumed by them and accepted by me that we were different from other people—no alcoholic beverages, no dancing, cards or theater, very little social life, and *much* work. I have a hard time convincing my children that even carbonated beverages had a faintly sinful aroma, and I remember my slight feeling of wickedness when I had my first bottle of "pop." We had good times together within the family, but we did not mix. So I was a pretty solitary boy, who read incessantly, and went all through high school with only two dates.

(2)   When I was twelve my parents bought a farm and we made our home there. The reasons were twofold. My father, having become a prosperous businessman, wanted it for a hobby. More important, I believe, was the fact that it seemed to my parents that a growing adolescent family should be removed from the "temptations" of suburban life.

(3)   Here I developed two interests which have probably had some real bearing on my later work. I became fascinated by the great night-flying moths (Gene Stratten-Porter's books were then in vogue), and I became an authority on the gorgeous Luna Polyphemus Cecropia and other moths which inhabited our woods. I laboriously bred the moths in captivity, reared the caterpillars, kept the cocoons over the long winter months, and in general realized some of the joys and frustrations of the scientist as he tries to observe nature.

(4)   My father was determined to operate his new farm on a scientific basis, so he bought many books on scientific agriculture. He encouraged his boys to have independent and profitable ventures of our own, so my brothers and I had a flock of chickens, and at one time or other reared from infancy lambs, pigs and calves. In doing this I became a student of scientific agriculture, and have only realized in recent years what a fundamental feeling for science I gained in that way. There was no one to tell me that Morison's *Feeds and Feeding* was not a book for a fourteen-year-old, so I ploughed through its hundreds of pages, learning how experiments were conducted—how control groups were matched with experimental groups, so that the influence of a given food on meat production or milk production could be established. I learned how difficult it is to test a hypothesis. I acquired a knowledge of and a respect for the methods of science in a field of practical endeavor.

College and Graduate Education
(5)   I started in college at Wisconsin in the field of agriculture. One of the things I remember best was the vehement statement of an agronomy professor in regard to the learning and use of facts. He stressed the futility of an encyclopedic knowledge for its own sake, and wound up with the injunction, "Don't be a damned ammunition wagon; be a rifle!"
(6)   During my first two college years my professional goal changed as the result of some emotionally charged student religious conferences, from that of a scientific agriculturist to that of the ministry—a slight shift! I changed from agriculture to history, believing this would be better preparation.
(7)   In my junior year I was selected as one of a dozen students from this country to go to China for an International World Student Christian Federation Conference. This was a most important experience for me. It was 1922, four years after the close of World War I. I saw how bitterly the French and Germans still hated each other, even though as individuals they seemed very likable. I was forced to stretch my thinking, to realize that sincere and honest people could believe in very divergent religious doctrines. In major ways I, for the first time, emancipated myself from the religious thinking of my parents, and realized that I could not go along with them. This independence of thought caused

great pain and stress in our relationship, but looking back on it I believe that here, more than at any other time, I became an independent person. Of course there was much revolt and rebellion in my attitude during that period, but the essential split was achieved during the six months I was on this trip to the Orient, and hence was thought through, away from the influence of home.

(8)   Although this is an account of elements which influenced my professional development rather than my personal growth, I wish to mention briefly one profoundly important factor in my personal life. It was at about the time of my trip to China that I fell in love with a lovely girl whom I had known for many years, even in childhood, and we were married, with the very reluctant consent of our parents, as soon as I finished college, in order that we could go to graduate school together. I cannot be very objective about this, but her steady and sustaining love and companionship during all the years since has been a most important and enriching factor in my life.

Underline new vocabulary in the reading. Try to find categories to organize the words. Write the words in the following box by category.

New words

Compare your categories with those of your classmates. Explain the reasons that you put words in those categories.

Exercise 3. Writing summary statements   Reread each paragraph of "This Is Me." Then for each paragraph, write a summary statement that gives the main idea of the paragraph. The statement should be just one sentence long. Paragraph 1 has been done for you as an example.

Paragraph 1

Rogers grew up in a large, strict and religious family, which was very close.

_____

Paragraph 2

_____

_____

Paragraph 3

_____

_____

Paragraph 4

_____

_____

Paragraph 5

_____

_____

Paragraph 6

_____

_____

Paragraph 7

_____

_____

Paragraph 8

_____

_____

Compare your summary statements with the statements of the people in your group. Decide for each paragraph who in the group has written the best summary statement.

  Exercise 4. Interviewing Carl Rogers   Carl Rogers was a very famous U.S. psychologist who had a great influence on U.S. education in the latter part of the twentieth century. His emphasis on understanding others as human beings and on education as a process of personal self-realization had a strong effect on teachers, school curricula, and the way educators talked about education. Knowing that Rogers became a famous humanistic psychologist, and having read the excerpt from "This Is Me," prepare a set of questions for Rogers. Make notes from each paragraph of the reading. Use the notes to form questions to ask of Rogers.

Notes

Exercise 5. Preparing an autobiography Brainstorm the topics below as they apply to your own life.

Birth	
Family	
Childhood	
Interests	
Friends	
Adolescence	
Heroes and Heroines	
Education	
Sports and Hobbies	
Crises and Problems	
Hopes and Dreams	

Talk about your life category by category. Add to your notes if new points emerge.

Exercise 6. Writing your thesis statement   Based on your notes and discussions, write a title that will capture your readers' attention and will introduce this autobiographical essay.

Title: _____

Now write a *general* statement about yourself. This will be the thesis statement of your introductory paragraph. The paragraphs of the body of your essay will support and develop this idea.

Thesis statement: _____

_____

_____

 Share your title and thesis statements. Are you sure they say what you want to write about? Do they express *you*? If not, change them.

Revised title: _____

Revised thesis statement: _____

_____

_____

 Exercise 7. Organizing the body of your essay   Look back at the notes you wrote in Exercise 3 and consider how they relate to your thesis. Decide which ideas you would like to develop; you do not need to include everything. Complete the following map on page 24 to help you organize.

a. Write each main idea in a separate circle. For example, if hopes and dreams are significant in explaining *you*, write *hopes and dreams* in one circle. This will become one body paragraph.

b. Write supporting details for each main idea and the lines radiating from each circle. You do not need to write on each line or you can add more lines if necessary.

c. Consider if there is a logical order for your paragraphs. There may be a chronological order or some topics may be of greater importance. Number the paragraphs in the order you would like to develop them in your essay.

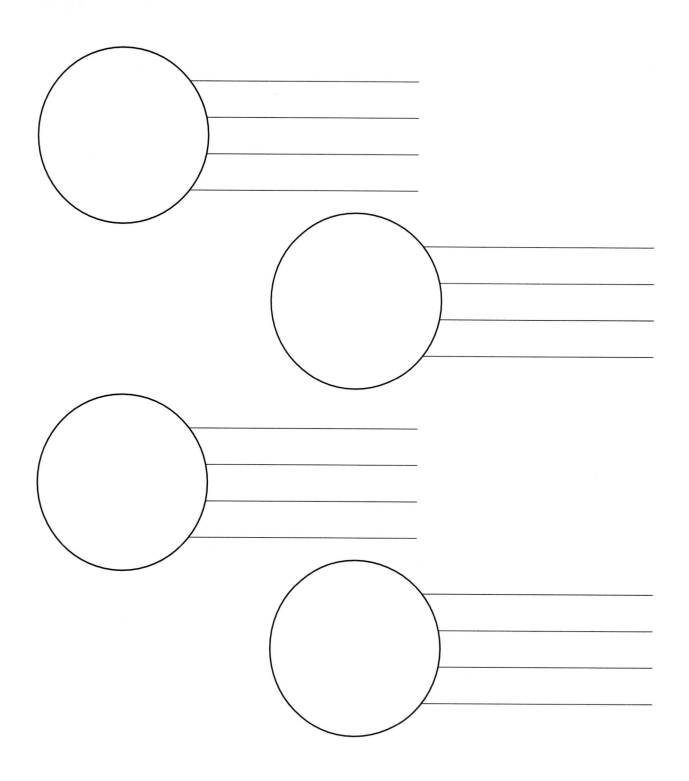

Exercise 8. Writing your first draft   Write the first draft of your essay. Use a word processor, if possible. Feel free to make changes in your title, thesis, or body as you write. Follow these guidelines.

a. Title—It should be interesting! It should be centered, capitalized, and punctuated correctly. Refer to Appendix VII for guidelines.

b. Introductory paragraph–It should interest or "hook" the reader. Refer to Appendix VIII for suggestions. It should include a clear thesis statement.

c. Body paragraphs—Each paragraph should have a clear topic sentence and supporting sentences.

d. Concluding paragraph—Summarize your essay by restating the main points you wanted to make about yourself. Refer to Appendix VIII for suggestions.

Reread your paper two times. The first time, check to see that your essay includes everything that you want to say about yourself and that it is clearly organized. The second time, check for spelling and grammar errors.

Exercise 9. Peer editing   Read a classmate's paper carefully, copy the following chart, complete it, and return it to your classmate with his or her essay.

Name: _____   Title: _____

Thesis: _____

1st Body Paragraph

    Main idea: _____

    _____

2nd Body Paragraph

    Main idea: _____

    _____

3rd Body Paragraph

    Main idea: _____

    _____

(Continued)

4th Body Paragraph (if there are four)

　　Main idea: _____

　　　　　　 _____

Conclusion:

Copy the last sentence here: _____

_____

What I like about this essay: _____

_____

_____

_____

One suggestion for improvement: _____

_____

_____

If you cannot complete the chart, discuss it with the writer. Now revise your essay before handing it in to your instructor.

D Journal Assignment

As you work through this unit, think about your life up to now. Each day write for fifteen minutes about some past experience in your life. Try to think about important things that happened to you.

Write a response to one of the following quotations.

"A friend is one who knows us, but loves us anyway."

—Fr. Jerome Cummings

"A joyful heart is the inevitable result of a heart burning with love."

—Mother Theresa

"Hold fast to dreams
For if dreams die
Life is a broken-winged bird
That cannot fly."

—Langston Hughes

Family and Relationships

A Prewriting

Exercise 1. Family trees   A family tree is a visual representation of a person's family. Here is an example of Monica Mason's family tree.

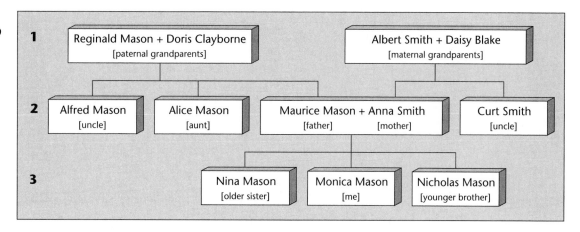

1	Reginald Mason + Doris Clayborne [paternal grandparents]		Albert Smith + Daisy Blake [maternal grandparents]	
2	Alfred Mason [uncle]	Alice Mason [aunt]	Maurice Mason + Anna Smith [father] [mother]	Curt Smith [uncle]
3		Nina Mason [older sister]	Monica Mason [me] Nicholas Mason [younger brother]	

A. With your partner, discuss the relationship between each pair of people in Monica's family. Here are some words you might need.

Line 1: son-in-law, daughter-in-law, in-laws

Line 2: brother-in-law, sister-in-law, aunt, uncle

Line 3: niece, nephew

Alfred Mason, Alice Mason, and Curt Smith are aunt and uncles to Nina, Monica, and Nicholas. If Alfred has a son, what relation would the son be to Nina, Monica, and Nicholas?

(It is the same word for a daughter.)

Answer _____

B. Draw your family tree by putting yourself in the center, your parents above you, brothers and sisters on the same line as you, aunts and uncles on the same line as your parents, and grandparents above your parents. Connect all the people with lines. Then discuss your tree with your partner. Use this opportunity to elaborate, or explain in more detail, and to ask your partner questions. Draw in the space provided on page 30.

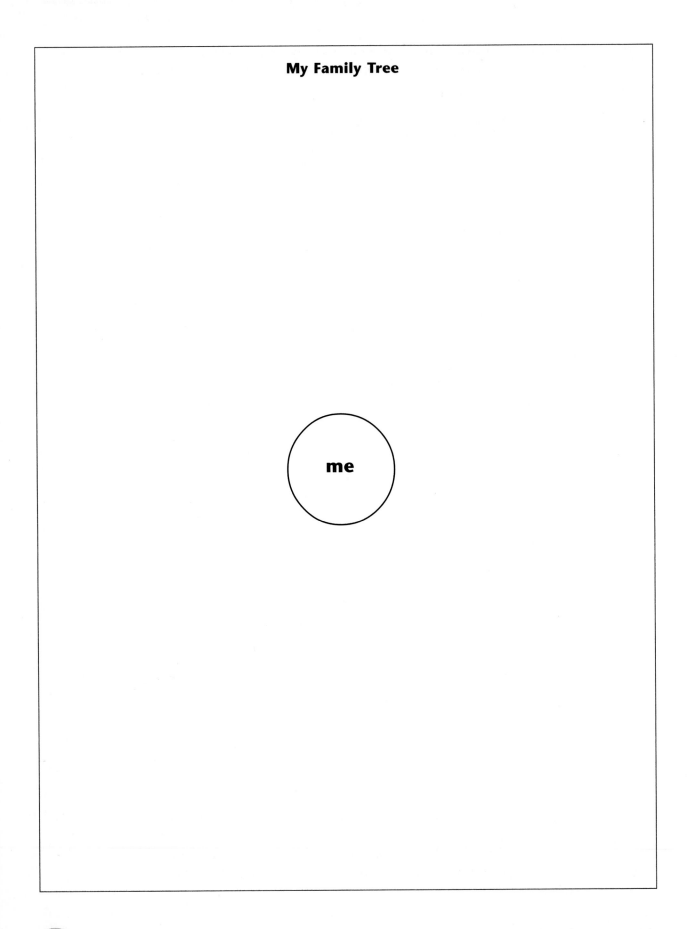

My Family Tree

me

Writing to Learn: *The Essay*

Exercise 2. In our family—a quick-write Begin writing with the words that follow. Continue writing for ten minutes. Don't worry about spelling, grammar, or punctuation. Just write freely and quickly. Write whatever comes into your mind.

In our family _____

_____

_____

_____

_____

_____

_____

_____

_____

_____

_____

_____

_____

_____

_____

_____

_____

_____

_____

_____

_____

 Now read some or all of your quick-write to a partner. Use this opportunity to elaborate, or explain in more detail, and to ask your partner questions.

Exercise 3. My favorite relative Think about your favorite relative: an aunt, an uncle, a cousin, a grandparent. Check off the reasons in the following list that correspond to why you respect or love that person so much.

My favorite _____   _____
                     (relationship)   (name)

_____   understands me very well.

_____   knows what I'm thinking.

_____   is always kind to me.

_____   buys me lots of things.

_____   shares adventures with me.

_____   raised me instead of my parents raising me.

_____   taught me how to . . .

_____   told me stories about life.

_____   gave me the values I live by.

_____   makes me laugh.

_____   is my best friend.

_____   is/was professionally successful.

_____   is/was always there for me.

_____   is kind, sweet, and sympathetic.

_____   is strong, honest, and understanding.

Now add a few other reasons of your own.

_____   _____

_____   _____

_____   _____

Now introduce your favorite relative to your group by telling the group what the person's name is, how old the person is, where he or she lives, and what he or she does in life. Then talk about the reasons you love that relative. For each reason, think of an example to illustrate your point.

Exercise 4. Sociogram A sociogram is a simple diagram of concentric circles that is used to illustrate the closeness of relationships. While a family tree illustrates formal relationships, a sociogram represents the closeness of these relationships. In the inner circle is you, and in the next circle are the people closest to you. Make your own sociogram below.

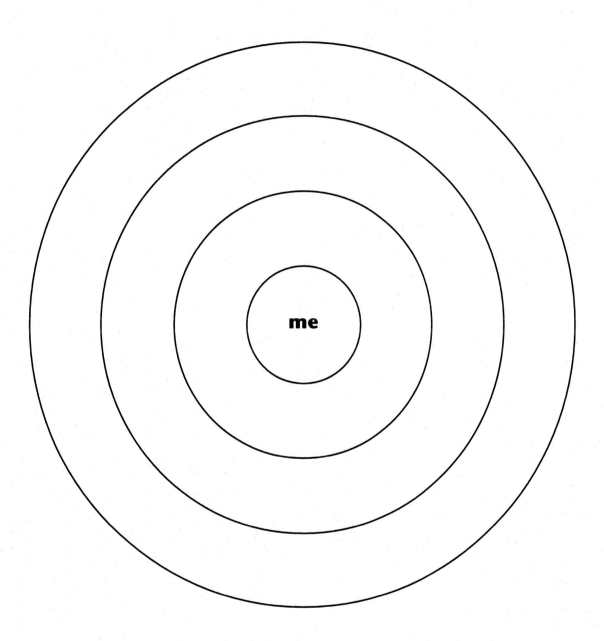

Now write about the sociogram. Describe the people in your life and their closeness to you. Explain how and why they are close to you.

<table>
<tr><td></td></tr>
</table>

_____

_____

_____

_____

_____

_____

_____

_____

_____

_____

_____

_____

_____

_____

_____

_____

_____

_____

Exercise 5. "When You Are Old" Young people rarely think a lot about being old. However, each of us will get old. This poem by the Irish poet William Butler Yeats is a poem about love—a love remembered in old age.

Listen to your instructor read the poem. Feel the rhythm and melody of the language. Feel the longing and nostalgia in the poet's words.

"When You Are Old"
W. B. Yeats

When you are old and grey and full of sleep,
And nodding by the fire, take down this book,
And slowly read, and dream of the soft look
Your eyes once had, and of their shadows deep;

How many loved your moments of glad grace,
And loved your beauty with love false or true,
But one man loved the pilgrim soul in you,
And loved the sorrows of your changing face;

And bending down beside the glowing bars,
Murmur, a little sadly, how love fled
And paced upon the mountains overhead
And hid his face among a crowd of stars.

Reread the poem and write vocabulary under each of the categories in the following box.

Movement:

Happiness or sadness:

Color/brightness or darkness:

 Talk about the meaning of the poem. Who is speaking? To whom? What mood does the poet create? Do you like the poem? Why or why not.

Exercise 6. When I am old Now think of yourself as an old person. Use your imagination to look many years into the future. You have had a full life. What have you done? Whom have you loved? What memories do you have? What regrets do you have? Make notes in the space provided.

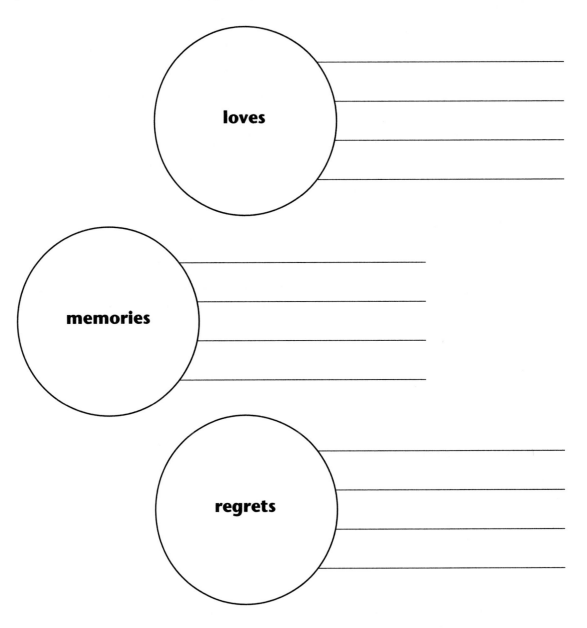

Now tell your partner about your life. Remember to use past tense to describe what happened in the past.

Writing to Learn: *The Essay*

B Structure

Writing Noun Clauses

A noun clause is a clause that acts grammatically as a noun. Using noun clauses broadens the variety of written expression of nouns. A noun clause often begins with a **relative pronoun:** *that, which(ever), who(ever), whom(ever), whose, when(ever), where(ever), why, how(ever), what(ever), whether, if.*

EXAMPLES:

Which one do you like?
interrogative pronoun + indefinite pronoun

⇒ I don't know *which one I like.*
noun clause becomes the object of verb *know*

Her writing was quite emotional.
possessive pronoun + gerund

⇒ *What she wrote* was quite emotional.
gerund becomes a noun clause subject of *was*

He is a fine athlete.
pronoun

⇒ *That he is a fine athlete* is clear.
the entire sentence becomes a noun clause subject of the verb *is*

This sentence can also be reversed.

⇒ It is clear *(that) he is a fine athlete.*
the noun clause becomes a subject compliment; *that* is often omitted

In quoted or reported speech, noun clauses are the objects of verbs of speaking. When the change is made from quoted to indirect speech, it is most common in formal writing to change each tense to its appropriate past tense.

Michael said, *"There's no running water."*
statement—noun clause with verb in present

⇒ Michael said *(that) there was no running water.*
statement—noun clause with verb in past

Ryan asked, *"Did you play volleyball?"*
question—noun clause with verb in past

⇒ Ryan asked *if I had played volleyball.*
question—noun clause with verb in past perfect

In ordinary conversation and in informal writing, it is acceptable to leave the verb tense unchanged.

EXAMPLE: Ryan asked *if I played volleyball.*

Notice that in the fourth example the word *that* is optional as an introducer of the noun clause. However, in the fifth example, the word *if* is required to express a yes/no question in reported speech.

Exercise 1. Recognizing noun clauses Underline the noun clauses in the sentences that follow.

> **EXAMPLE:** I didn't understand <u>what the teacher said to me.</u>

1. I know what your brother does for a living.

2. They don't know if they should invite their in-laws.

3. Kim says that almost all Koreans have extended families.

4. Mom shouted to us that it was time for dinner.

5. What his wife was singing was a Beatles' song.

6. I wonder whose sister-in-law she is.

7. Tell me why your aunt can't come to the wedding.

8. My great uncle learned how to ski.

9. Their children asked whether they were buying a new car.

10. Whoever wants to meet lots of new people should come to our family reunion.

 Exercise 2. Creating sentences with noun clauses Create a sentence using each noun clause that follows. Use the examples and practice sentences seen thus far in the Structure section for ideas. When you finish, compare your work with another pair's work.

> **EXAMPLE:** that I would fall in love soon
> *The fortune teller predicted that I would fall in love soon.*

1. whoever wants to have children

2. whether you come to the wedding

3. why the family doesn't get together more

4. if the whole family is invited

5. where my uncle lives

6. whose grandson he is

Exercise 3. Creating sentences with noun clauses introduced by *that* and noun phrases with infinitives and gerunds

> # Noun Clauses with *That*
>
> Some clauses with *that* are noun clauses. Some phrases with *infinitives* and *gerunds* are noun phrases. Look at these sentences. Notice that in these examples the noun clause acts as object of the main verb in the sentence.
>
> **EXAMPLES:**   that   My students know *that I play the guitar.*
>   noun clause
>
>   infinitive   My wife asked *me to play guitar for her.*
>   noun phrase
>
>   gerund   My wife knows *playing guitar keeps me happy.*
>   noun phrase

Rewrite the sentences that follow into sentences with noun clauses or noun phrases. You can think of your own words to complete each sentence or choose from some of the completions listed here.

> **EXAMPLES:** Marriage is the norm in U.S. society.
>
> **That marriage is the norm in U.S. society** *doesn't mean many*
>   noun clause   *couples live together without getting married.*
>
> It is still the norm **to get married in U.S. society.**
>   noun phrase
>
> **Getting married** *is still the norm in U.S. society.*
> noun phrase

1. Divorce is common in many countries.

   _____

2. A good relationship is not easy to achieve.

   _____

3. The birth rate has actually dropped in several countries.

   _____

4. There are many widows in the United States.

   _____

5. Remarriage is a solution for widowers.

_____

6. Many children live in blended families.

_____

7. A single parent works and raises children.

_____

8. Lots of babies go to day care at less than a year old.

_____

Exercise 4. More practice with reported speech   Change the following questions to reported speech.

Reported Speech

Questions in reported speech can be difficult. You need to remember to change the verb tense, pronouns, and word order. Be sure that the noun clause does not have question word order.

EXAMPLE: She asked, "Where are you going?"

She asked me where I was going.

Notice that in yes/no questions *if* replaces the question word, and the pronouns, tense, and word order change.

EXAMPLE: She asked him, "Do you want to get married?"

She asked him if he wanted to get married.

1. Her mother asked her, "When are you going to get married?

_____

2. My cousin emailed me to ask, "Will you come and visit me?

_____

3. My sister-in-law asked, "Why did you do that?

_____

4. Sociologists ask themselves, "How can we accurately define the American family?"

_____

5. She asked me, "Do you know what you really want?"

_____

6. The student inquired, "Where can I find the answer to that question?"

_____

7. They wanted to know, "Why did you say that?"

_____

8. His parents asked him, "Will you come home for the holidays?"

_____

 Exercise 5. "The Borzhomi Nose" Read this excerpt from a short story by Harrison Powers. You will notice that the text is marked with two asterisks (*). The original quotation marks have been deleted in the section between the asterisks. After you reread the story, add quotation marks where needed.

"The Borzhomi Nose"
Harrison Powers

My mother has only been in the United States for a few months. She has lived all her life in a small mountain town in Georgia. Not Georgia, U.S.A. My mother is from the Georgia that's in the Soviet Union.

We were separated when I was very young. The details aren't important. But I grew up in the States while my mother remained in Russia. Now that she is here with me, I feel she should enjoy all the good things she has missed. And to my mind, the main thing is baseball.

I have been a baseball fan all my life. I love the game. "Baseball," I said to myself, "will really show Mama what America is like."

When I told her I would take her to a game, she seemed pleased.

"I like games," she said.

"Good. Nothing is too good for my Mama." I kissed her cheek. "I got box seats."

She seemed disappointed.

---

*

What's the matter, Mama? I asked.

It's nothing, she said. It's just I'm not so young anymore. I'm afraid I couldn't sit on a box.

Then her face lit up. She had an idea. We could bring folding chairs from the porch, she said.

I explained the seats would be good enough. A little hard maybe, but all right.

When we got there, Mama was pleased with the crowds and the noise. She held tightly to my arm. In her free hand, she carried a large bag. Her purse, I told myself, won't do for America. I decided to buy her a new one.

We settled in our seats. Mama asked, Would you like something to eat? She opened the huge bag. It wasn't her purse after all. It turned out to be a traveling refrigerator.

The bag contained a two-foot salami, two kinds of bread, three tomatoes, six boiled eggs, a head of lettuce, and a large bottle of apple cider. There was mustard, relish, ketchup, and horseradish.

I had a pie, she said sadly. It wouldn't fit. We can have it when we get home. We'll probably be hungry.

But Mama, I said. I wanted to buy you the food here. They have hot dogs, popcorn, potato chips, soda, everything.

They have salami and good black bread? Tomatoes?
*

I had to admit they didn't.

"So eat and enjoy it," she said. She turned to the man beside her. "Hey mister. You want a salami sandwich?"

By the time Mama finished making sandwiches, it was the end of the third inning. Everybody had salami and apple cider. We were getting dirty looks from the guy selling hot dogs. A woman behind me asked for more mustard.

Bruce Collins opened the forth inning with a home run. The crowd was on its feet cheering. Mama put down her groceries and stood up to see.

"What is it?" she asked.

"A home run, Mama. The batter just made a home run." I was all excited.

"So why is there such a fuss if he had to run home a minute?" She looked puzzled. Then she saw something of greater interest.

Now rewrite the noun phrases of direct speech into indirect speech.

EXAMPLE: I told myself that baseball would really show Mama what America was like.

_____

_____

_____

_____

_____

_____

_____

_____

_____

_____

_____

_____

_____

_____

 Exercise 6. Recording a conversation Harrison Powers re-created a conversation between his mother and himself. Think about a recent conversation you had with your mother, father, brother, sister, or other relative. Write it in direct speech on the next page. You probably don't remember exactly what was said, so use a little imagination. Reinvent the conversation. Remember to do the following:

1. use quotation marks to show direct speech, and

2. begin a new paragraph each time there is a new speaker.

_____

_____

_____

_____

_____

_____

_____

_____

_____

_____

_____

_____

_____

_____

_____

_____

_____

 Exercise 7. Conversation exchange   Exchange books. Rewrite your partner's conversation with a relative on a separate sheet of paper. Use indirect speech. Remember to do the following:

1. shift tense if necessary, and

2. remove quotation marks.

Writing to Learn: *The Essay*

C Writing and Editing

Exercise 1. What you remember Think about your family, relatives, and friends. What is distinctive about each person? Is it big dark eyes? Or maybe it's the way they are always smiling and happy? Each person has some personality trait or some physical attribute that we remember. Some of those close to us may have done something that we will never forget. Perhaps they gave us a precious gift or told us a story by which we live our lives. In the following chart, list the person and what makes him or her memorable for you.

EXAMPLES:	my mother	dark curly hair
	my brother	always upbeat and optimistic
	my grandfather	played the piano and sang every Sunday after dinner

Person	Memory
My older sister	Her room was always filled with pictures of Elvis Presley.

Now take turns in your group talking about these people. When you listen to your classmate speak, ask questions for clarification and information.

EXAMPLE: My best friend ran the Boston Marathon!

Really? How long did it take her? Will she do it again?

Exercise 2. "Hands That Held a Family Together" Read this award-winning essay by Di Yin Lu, who was a high school student in the Bronx, New York, when she wrote this essay.

"Hands That Held a Family Together"
Di Yin Lu

I remember my grandmother by her hands and feet. Not because there is anything wrong with the rest of her—my grandmother has aged gracefully—but because her hands and feet are her most striking features.

Against her willowy frame her broad hands with the bulging knuckles look like a mistake. Her disproportionately small feet would be more fitting on a baby than on a grown woman. But despite their size, her feet have carried her through wars, her hands have worked her out of poverty, and I admire them.

I can see her now, a slim girl of 12, stifling a scream with her hand as her mother crams her feet into a pair of three-inch shoes. According to turn-of-the-century Chinese mothers, men will not marry girls whose feet are bigger than their own hands; such large feet aren't ladylike.

I hear the soft pitter-patter of my grandma's feet as she paces along a wooden dock, waiting for her husband to return from Burma; the hollow wrapping of her fists against police department doors after Red Army soldiers arrested her husband during the Communist Revolution.

I see her fingers flying as she pulls a needle in and out of silk handkerchiefs, splashing the white surface with brilliant threads that grow into ducks, flowers, and calligraphy. Grandma pawned her needlework for food after the Communists took her husband to jail, and kept her sons from dying of starvation at a time when gold wasn't worth more than the cracked floorboards beneath her feet.

I see her feet, bruised and swollen from walking in an old pair of cloth shoes, from one pawn shop to another. I feel her hands grow coarse and stiff from dyeing threads in the winter. But she keeps walking, and sewing, and selling.

I feel her fingers slipping a thin jade ring onto mine the morning before I leave for America. The plane is delayed because of a thunderstorm, and my parents are busy talking to friends on the other side of Gate 86. Grandma leans heavily on her cane, holding my hand, the one with the ring on it. I remember feeling her hand tremble, and asking her to sit down because I knew her feet hurt on rainy days. She squeezes my hand so hard the ring leaves an imprint on both our fingers.

I look through the photographs and see a grandma who is fading away. Her eyes caved deeper and deeper into her face, her skin slackened until it looks like it would tear apart at a touch. But that is not how I will remember her. My memories are of faltering steps, of strong grips, of soft hand-embroidered handkerchiefs.

This essay contains a lot of descriptive language, some of it difficult. Write new words in the space provided. Write phrases, rather than isolated words, and define or give synonyms.

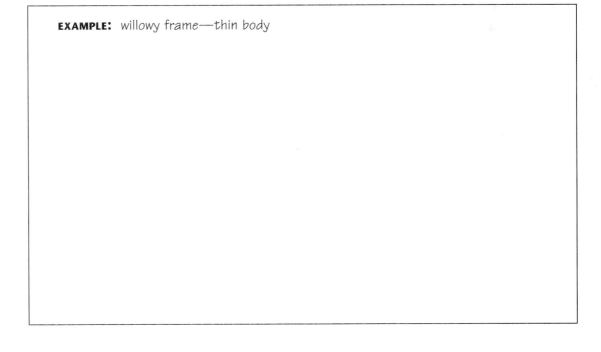

EXAMPLE: willowy frame—thin body

Exercise 3. A letter to Grandma—quick-write Pretend that you are Di Yin. You are writing a letter to your grandma. Start off with "Dear Grandma." Then just write whatever comes into your mind. Your instructor will tell you when to stop writing.

Now exchange books with your partner. Read your partner's quick-write. Did you write about similar things? Did you use a similar tone (style and expression) in your writing?

Exercise 4. Considering the tone of the essay   Go back and reread the essay. Underline words and phrases that give you a feeling about the tone that writer takes. Copy them in the space provided.

What incidents in the grandmother's life strike you as sad? List them in the space provided. Notice that they add to the tone of the writing.

Exercise 5. Deciding on a topic for your essay You are going to write an essay about a person in which you stress the physical characteristics and character of your subject, just like Di Yin Lu did in her essay about her grandmother. The person you write about can be a family member, relative, or friend. The essay should take a clear tone: humorous, nostalgic, or grateful, for example. You should use description of events in the life of that person along with description of the person's character.

Step 1. Revisit Exercise 1 on page 45. Among the people you have listed, who is the one about whom you could write a lot? Who is the one who did things in ways you remember quite well? _____

What is that person's distinctive physical feature? _____

What is that person's character like? _____

Step 2. Look at the notes below, an elaboration of the example in Exercise 1.

My older sister

always smiling—eyes very big

always talking—very fast and loud—with excitement

cheerful

looks on the bright side

a little crazy or immature—not at all practical

devoted lifelong fan of Elvis

has all his records, tapes and CDs

kept an Elvis cardboard poster in her bedroom

went to her first Elvis concert when 16 years old

had lots of friends who were fans of Elvis

has visited Graceland many times

sat in the front row of his concerts

caught a few of Elvis's sweaty scarves at his concerts

has always believed in the goodness of others

treats those she loves with affection and humor

cried for days when Elvis died but bounced back to her normal cheerful self

devotion to Elvis borders on religious

From these notes, an essay can be constructed. The tone would be light and humorous. The defining physical characteristic would be the older sister's smile.

Step 3. Make notes for your essay in the space provided.

```
                          Notes




















```

What is the character of the person you are writing about? _____

_____

What physical characteristic will you emphasize? _____

What tone do you want to create? _____

Step 4. Read your notes to the people in your group. Ask them if they get a clear idea of a physical feature and the character of the person you have chosen to write about. If not, add more detail to your notes.

Exercise 6. Strengthening writing with details   You can improve your writing by supporting your thesis with a particular event or incident and dialogue. Think of an event that illustrates your thesis and write it after the following example.

EXAMPLE: Whenever there was a concert in the New York area, our house became the "hotel" for a dozen or so Elvis fans. I remember them arriving in "Love Me Tender" shirts, carrying their sleeping bags and cameras, and talking nonstop. It was something I looked forward to with the greatest anticipation while my parents dreaded each visit and wished he'd never perform in our state again.

Event:

_____

_____

_____

_____

_____

_____

Now think of a conversation that supports your thesis.

EXAMPLE: "Carol," I said, "James called, and he said he wants to come over tonight."

"Un-uh, can't do it," she said to my surprise. "I gotta go to my fan club meeting tonight."

"But you've been waiting for his call all week!" I couldn't believe she would turn down the guy she'd been after since school started.

"Too bad. He chose the wrong night. Elvis first!" And with that she grinned and pasted an Elvis photo into her scrapbook.

Writing to Learn: *The Essay*

Conversation:

_____

_____

_____

_____

_____

_____

_____

_____

_____

_____

_____

_____

_____

_____

_____

_____

_____

Exercise 7. Organizing to write Before writing, it is important to organize. One way to do that is to make a brief outline based on your notes.

EXAMPLE: Introduction: Hook—Conversation (see preceding)

Thesis: My older sister has always been frantically and enthusiastically happy and upbeat.

Body Paragraph 1: What her room looked like/what she collected

Body Paragraph 2: What she looked like/how she dressed

Body Paragraph 3: Her friends—other Elvis fans

Body Paragraph 4: What she's like as an adult—after his death

Conclusion: Why I love her as she is—add a last example

```
Introduction:  Hook: _____

               Thesis: _____

Body Paragraph 1: _____

Body Paragraph 2: _____

Body Paragraph 3: _____

Body Paragraph 4: _____

   Conclusion: _____
```

Note: The number of body paragraphs will depend on how you organize your ideas. You can have from two to six or more body paragraphs.

Exercise 8. Writing your essay   Now you're ready to write. Write your first draft on a piece of paper or on the computer. Remember to concentrate on establishing a tone for the essay. Be sure that all of your paragraphs support your thesis. Each paragraph needs a topic sentence or controlling idea and adequate support.

Exercise 9. Revising your essay   Read your partner's essay and answer these questions.

1. Who is the subject of the essay? _____

2. What is the tone of the essay? _____

3. What is the distinguishing characteristic of this person? _____

4. Is the essay well developed?   yes _____   no _____

5. Is there something in the essay that does not fit?   yes _____   no _____

   Explain _____

6. Does the reader need more information?   yes _____   no _____

   About what? _____

Consider the feedback from your partner. Make any changes you feel you should make before turning the essay in to your instructor.

D Journal Assignment

Write about each of the following:

■ Think about a gift that a member of your family gave you. That gift could be something that was wrapped in a package, or it could be an experience or a lesson. Write about it.

■ Imagine that one of your parents is writing about you. What would he or she write?

■ Reread the story of "The Borzhomi Nose" on pages 41–42. The story is not complete. What did Mama see that was so interesting? Write the ending of the story.

■ Write a response to one or more of the following quotations.

"The family is one of nature's masterpieces"
—George Santayana, *The Life of Reason*

"Happiness is having a large, loving, caring, close-knit family in another city."
—George Burns

"A father may turn his back on his child, brother and sisters may become inveterate enemies, husbands may desert their wives, wives their husbands, but a mother's love endures through all."
—Washington Irving

"Every man must define his identity against his mother. If he does not, he falls back into her and is swallowed up."
—Camille Paglia

Education

A   Prewriting

Exercise 1. Making lists   In many parts of North America, elementary school includes kindergarten through grade six (K–6). Secondary school is often divided into two parts: junior high school (7–8) and high school (9–12). A first course of study in college can be two years at a community college or four years at college or university.

The next page contains words and phrases that you can associate with these three different levels of schooling. Put the words and phrases into the list that follows them. Use your own reasons for doing so. You may put an item in more than one list. If there are words that you do not know, use your dictionary or ask your teacher.

cafeteria playground recess **toys** crossing guard teacher

final exams principal candy cheating music class **professor**

essay **textbook** cutting class boyfriend/girlfriend pop quiz

backpack dean schoolbag

diploma president **beer** club best friend student center

cigarettes teammate gum school trip calculus

parent's permission cutting and pasting **prom**

geometry college entrance exams taking notes at a lecture **arithmetic**

spring break birthday party achievement tests

Elementary school	Secondary school	College/University

Now add two more words to each column. Then, compare and explain your lists.

Exercise 2. Talking about school   Choose one of the three levels of schooling to discuss. Talk about schooling at that level in your country. Prepare a two-minute talk for your group in which you use most or all of the words and phrases that you copied into the chart in Exercise 1 on page 57. Make notes for your talk in the space provided. Answer questions after you speak.

Notes

Exercise 3. Shirley's pledge   The following excerpt is from the book *In the Year of the Boar and Jackie Robinson.* In this excerpt, a young immigrant girl participates with her class in the Pledge of Allegiance without fully understanding; she hears the words that she knows. Before reading it, listen to your teacher read the pledge that Shirley heard and misunderstood.

"I pledge allegiance to the flag of the United States of America. And to the Republic for which it stands, one nation under God, indivisible with liberty and justice for all."

From *In the Year of the Boar and Jackie Robinson*
by Bette Bao Lord

Finally Mrs. Rappaport cleared her throat, and the room was still. With hands over hearts, the class performed the ritual that ushered in another day at school.

Shirley's voice was lost in the chorus.

"I pledge a lesson to the frog of the United States of America, and to the wee puppet for witches' hands. One Asian, in the vestibule, with little tea and just rice for all."

Make a list of the words that Shirley misunderstood. Across from each word, write the word she should have said.

Shirley's words	The Pledge of Allegiance
a lesson	allegiance

Talk about the rituals in your elementary or high school. Did you salute a flag or sing a song? If yes, was the ritual patriotic, religious, or instructional? Do you remember the words? How did you feel at that time?

Exercise 4. Quick-write We all have memories that stand out. When you think about your high school years, you may remember a school activity such as lunch time, math class, or a sport or club. You may remember a particular teacher or classmate. You may remember a particular embarrassing or humorous experience, or a time when you were sad or proud. Close your eyes for a moment and think. Then write as much as you can in five minutes on this topic.

When I think about my high school years, I remember clearly _____

_____

_____

_____

_____

_____

_____

_____

_____

_____

_____

_____

_____

_____

_____

_____

_____

_____

_____

_____

_____

_____

 Read your quick-write to your group. Listen carefully as your group mates read. As each person speaks, write a few key words to help you remember what you want to ask about or comment on.

Exercise 5. Visualizing a classroom In *Among Schoolchildren,* Tracy Kidder follows the school year of Chris Zajac, a fourth grade teacher in Holyoke, Massachusetts. Chris organizes her room for teaching just before the school year begins. Read the following excerpt and demonstrate your comprehension by sketching the classroom described. Draw in the space provided on page 62.

From *Among Schoolchildren*
by Tracy Kidder

Chris looked around her empty classroom. It was fairly small as classrooms go, about twenty-five feet by thirty-six feet.

She put up bulletin board displays, scouted up pencils and many kinds of paper—crayons hadn't yet arrived; she'd borrowed some of her son's—made a red paper apple for her door, and moved the desks around into the layout she had settled on in her first years of teaching. She didn't use the truly ancient arrangement, with the teacher's desk up front and the children's in even rows before it. Her desk was already where she wanted it, in a corner by the window. She had to be on her feet and moving in order to teach. Over there in the corner, her desk wouldn't get in her way. And she could retire to it in between lessons, at a little distance from the children, and still see down the hallway between her door and the boys' room—a strategic piece of real estate—and also keep an eye on all the children at their desks. She pushed most of the children's small, beige-topped desks side by side, in a continuous perimeter describing three-quarters of a square, open at the front. She put four desks in the middle of the square, so that each of those four had space between it and any other desk. These were Chris's "middle-person desks," where it was especially hard to hide, although even the back row of the perimeter was more exposed than back rows usually are.

When the room was arranged to her liking, she went home to the last days of summer.

Chris's classroom

Exercise 6. Describing your classroom   Now think about one of your
elementary school classrooms. What did the classroom look like? How were things
organized? Where did the students sit? Where was the teacher's desk? What was in
the classroom besides desks and chairs? If it helps, you might want to make a
sketch of how that classroom looked.

My classroom

Now write for ten minutes about that classroom.

_____

_____

_____

_____

_____

_____

_____

_____

_____

_____

_____

_____

_____

_____

_____

_____

_____

_____

_____

_____

_____

 Show your picture to your classmates while you read your description.

Exercise 7. Remembering your school experience Close your eyes and imagine that you are back in that classroom. You are sitting at your desk on the first day of a new school year. How do you feel? What thoughts are going through your mind? What are you wondering about your new teacher? What are you wondering about what you will study?

Now write for ten minutes about your feelings.

_____

_____

_____

_____

_____

_____

_____

_____

_____

_____

_____

_____

_____

_____

_____

_____

_____

_____

_____

_____

_____

_____

Read your quick-write to your group. As your group mates read, write down adjectives that describe their feelings.

Name _____   Adjectives _____

Name _____   Adjectives _____

Name _____   Adjectives _____

B   S t r u c t u r e

Exercise 1. How to be a good college teacher   Students know a great deal about what makes a good teacher. Brainstorm advice on how to be a good college teacher. Take five minutes to write your ideas in the following box.

Now share ideas with the entire class and make a comprehensive list on the board.

Writing to Learn: *The Essay*

Exercise 2. "A Guide to Teaching"   Now read the following excerpt from the editorial of a college newspaper, *The Channels*.

A Guide to Teaching

Remember your favorite teacher?

Maybe it was second grade, when you got scratch-and-sniff stickers on your homework. Maybe it was seventh grade, when you set off rockets on the soccer field and realized you wanted to be a scientist. Maybe it was sophomore year in high school, when you played the teacher's special addition of Jeopardy to learn about the American Revolution.

We remember our favorite teachers because they were unique. They had a way of making class interesting.

How do they do it? How do they reach those eager young minds waiting to be molded? *The Channels* editorial board polled itself and came up with a few suggestions:

Introduce yourself at the beginning of the semester. If you don't tell students your name and what to call you, they won't know your name and they won't call you.

Get to know your students. Learn their names, especially in small classes. If you take an interest in them, they're more apt to take an interest in your class.

Be organized. If you don't know what you're doing during the semester, students won't know what you're doing. If you aren't clear about your expectations, students certainly won't meet them.

Keep your office hours. They need help. They get confused. They seek guidance. If you're not there when they need you, you're not completing your end of the bargain.

Find new ways of giving information. You're teaching Generation MTV. If you don't make an attempt to entertain, you're not reaching students. It can be as simple as telling a joke, or telling a personal story, or making references students understand—to the movies they see, the music they listen to, the hobbies they enjoy.

Involve students in class discussions. Give them the opportunity to share their opinions. Ask them to share their experiences. Give points to students for their contributions. If they participate, they learn from each other.

Don't show up to class late. If you do it, they'll do it. Set a good example. If you don't come to class at all, neither will they.

Don't teach in only one learning style. Remember that everyone learns differently. Some need to hear; some need to see; some need to read; some need to do. If you teach in only one style, you are excluding many of your students.

[. . .]

Teaching is more than regurgitating information, particularly at the college level. Teachers and students need to be partners in education. They share a common goal: learning. A teacher can make anything, even the most mundane of topics, appeal to students if they do it right.

Write new vocabulary words and an original sentence for each in the following box.

Vocabulary words

Writing to Learn: *The Essay*

Compare the list your class has put on the board with the recommendations in the editorial. You can do this by completing the Venn diagram.

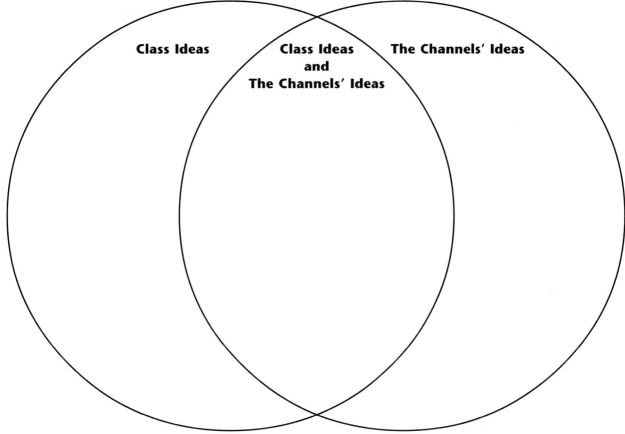

Class Ideas

Class Ideas and The Channels' Ideas

The Channels' Ideas

Now underline all the sentences in the reading that have an *if*-clause in them. Do they all have the same sense of meaning and time? Here are some questions to help you decide.

1. Are the sentences about the past, the present, or the future?

2. Are the sentences about facts, habits, or predictions?

3. Do the sentences give commands or advice, or refer to possibility?

 Exercise 3. Understanding conditional sentences   In English, there are many ways to express the *conditional* relationship between ideas. A conditional relationship is one in which the idea expressed in the main clause of the sentence is qualified in some way by what is expressed in the dependent clause of the sentence.

Conditional Constructions

In simple terms, there are three basic conditional constructions in English. They are often illustrated by sentences using *if.* Read each sentence. Then underline the main clause once and the dependent clause twice. (Remember that the dependent clause begins with *if.*)

1. You will remember the lecture better if you take notes.
2. I would record the lecture if I had a tape recorder.
3. I could have picked you up if I had known you were going to the lecture.

_____ Which sentence carries a strong prediction, almost like advice?

_____ Which sentence shows that the events have already happened?

_____ Which sentence shows that the opposite is actually true?

However, to say that English has three conditionals is oversimplifying the case. Read the following sentences. They all express conditionality.

_____ 1. If it were to rain, they would hold the graduation indoors.

_____ 2. If it rains, they will hold the graduation indoors.

_____ 3. I would have helped you clean up after the reception for the new professor if you had asked me.

_____ 4. My father would have been really proud if he could have attended my graduation.

_____ 5. If I had the time, I would rewrite my science paper.

_____ 6. They may go to Spain if the college runs the program this spring.

_____ 7. She might not want to take that class when she finds out who's teaching it.

_____ 8. If he failed the test, he can take it again.

_____ 9. If she took the test, she got an A, guaranteed.

_____ 10. She comes late to class whenever there's a paper due.

_____ 11. When a baby is around a year and a half years old, it begins to speak.

_____ 12. If you can't learn English in her class, you can't learn it anywhere.

- Notice how *if, when,* and *whenever* are used in conditional sentences.

- Notice that if any of these words begins the sentence, there is a comma after the end of the first clause.

- Notice that many different verb constructions can be used in conditional sentences.

English conditional sentences can be divided into sentences that are factual, sentences that are predictive of the future, and sentences that are imaginative.

Reread sentences 1 to 12. In the space next to each sentence, put an **F** if the sentence is factual; put a **P** if the sentence is predictive, or put an **I** if the sentence is imaginative.

EXAMPLE: ___I___ I would have passed the test if I hadn't been absent last week.

The sentence is imaginative because it did not happen. The speaker or writer did not pass the test. The person is imagining under what condition he or she would have passed it.

Exercise 4. Facts about the education system in your country Think about the education system in your country. At what age do you begin to study? What subjects do you need to study to enter university? What do you do if you don't have the money to study after secondary school? Write three factual statements about your country's education system using *if* or *when*.

EXAMPLE: Children start kindergarten when they are five years old.

If a child doesn't pay attention in class, the teacher can punish the child.

1. _____

2. _____

3. _____

Take turns reading your sentences to each other in your group. Then read one of your sentences to your instructor. Ask about the education system of his or her country.

EXAMPLE: Most adults go to private language schools if they want to learn English.

How about here?

Exercise 5. Predictive statements about student learning   Write three predictive statements about students and learning.

> **EXAMPLE:** *If you had a computer at home, it would be easier to complete your work and do research.*

1. _____

2. _____

3. _____

Exercise 6. Imaginative statements   Write three imaginative statements about teachers and learning.

> **EXAMPLE:** *If kindergarten teachers were better paid, we might not have a teacher shortage.*

1. _____

2. _____

3. _____

C   # Writing and Editing

Exercise 1. "Salam, Shalom"   The passage that follows comes from an article in *Teaching Tolerance* magazine. The article is about a bilingual Arabic-Hebrew school located in the village of *Wahat al-Salam* (Arabic) or *Neve Shalom* (Hebrew). It is an Arab-Israeli cooperative school that strives to create a place where Arabs and Israelis can study and play side by side.

From "Salam, Shalom"
by Ilene R. Prusher

"The best way to get to know someone is if we speak each other's language," says Boaz Kitain, the Jewish principal, as he oversees a noisy game of kickball during recess. Despite administrators' attempts to employ the two languages equally, down to every last poster and piece of artwork, the children are calling out to each other in Hebrew. On the playground and elsewhere outside of class, Hebrew is the lingua franca.

Kitain and his colleagues see this as a weakness. It's an imbalance that may be only natural in a state where most Arabs grow up learning Hebrew—overhearing it on television and radio and needing to use it in everyday communication—but Jews have few opportunities to learn Arabic and usually won't hear it at all. As a result, not only are the Jewish students at Neve Shalom weaker in Arabic, but few of the Jewish teachers are fluent in the language. The Arab students and teachers, on the other hand, are typically bilingual.

"We don't expect that the Jewish kids will know Arabic as well as the Arab kids learn Hebrew," Kitain says. "That's the reality. The goal is that they can understand each other and write on a basic level." Nonetheless, teachers recently began suspecting that some of their Jewish graduates were leaving the school without a proficiency in Arabic—and that Hebrew was becoming more dominant than they had hoped it would be.

In spite of the reality of living in a predominantly Jewish society, Diana Shalufe-Rizek, a 14 year resident of Neve Shalom who has taught Arabic language, art and culture classes at the school for the past six years, believes that everyone at Neve Shalom should be more open to learning both languages.

"Teaching here is hard," she says, "and what makes it so is that we try to be equal in languages, but we haven't succeeded because our kids see what is going on outside. As long as the Jewish teachers are unable to speak Arabic, the situation will continue.

"Why do the Palestinian children have to feel that to speak with the Jewish kids they must speak in Hebrew?" she asks. "This is a compromise. They have to be equal."

In response to the call for a language balance, the school's administrators decided last year that regardless of the subject studied, the first 20 minutes of every day would be devoted to speaking only Arabic.

Write new vocabulary words in the space provided on page 74.

Unit 3: Education

New vocabulary words

Notice in the reading that the words of the principal and then of the Arabic language teacher are followed by an elaboration of the points that they are making. For example, the principal says that the best way to get to know other people is to learn to speak their language. Then the writer gives more information about the attempt to use Arabic and Hebrew equally at *Wahat al-Salam,* or *Neve Shalom.* In this way, the rhythm of this passage from the story is created. Reread the passage. Look for direct speech. Then look for how the ideas in that speech are treated by the writer following the direct speech.

 Exercise 2. Quoting your classmates   Jot down a couple of questions to ask classmates about how people in their country learn English. For example, you might ask, *"In your country, do parents push their children to learn English because they want them to succeed?"* or *"Are there bilingual schools in your country that teach in your language and in English?"*

Questions:

1. _____

2. _____

3. _____

Now move around the room and interview some classmates. Write down their exact words to your questions. You might have to ask them to repeat what they said or to say it more slowly.

What my classmates said:

_____

_____

_____

_____

_____

_____

Exercise 3. Writing with quotations   Choose the most interesting quotation from a classmate you have written down. Go back to that classmate and ask for some more information that relates to his or her answer. Make notes on what is said. You don't need to write down the exact words this time.

Notes

Now write a paragraph using your classmate's words; then, elaborate on what he or she said by writing more sentences from your second interview. For example, Raoul from Colombia said, "In my country, middle class children often go to private bilingual schools where they study in Spanish and English."

Notes from talking to Raoul

public schools not as good   are monolingual Spanish

kids in bilingual schools start in pre-kindergarten

speak only in English the first two years

begin to study school subjects in English by elementary grades

move back to Spanish in high school to prepare
for national college entrance exam

"In my country, middle-class children often go to private bilingual schools where they study in Spanish and in English," says my classmate Raoul Martinez. Raoul is from Bogota, Colombia, and he is the product of a private bilingual Spanish-English education. Raoul says that most middle-class families send their children to private schools because the public education system is not as good as the private one. When he attended school, Raoul began as a pre-kindergarten student. He spoke only English in the classroom during his first two years. By the time he started the elementary grades, he was learning school subjects like math and science in English. However, by the time Raoul was ready to graduate high school, his education was mainly conducted in his native language, Spanish. This was because all high school students need to prepare for the national college entrance exams that are given in Spanish, except for the English language portion. Raoul's bilingual education has prepared him very well to study in English.

Write your paragraph in the space provided on page 77.

Exercise 4. Developing a paragraph into an essay Just like a paragraph, an essay has a beginning, a middle, and an end. In the paragraph, we look for a strong opening, often called a hook. A quotation is an excellent hook. We can also use a hook to start the first paragraph of an essay.

Next in the paragraph we look for a topic sentence (which could be the hook) and development of the topic sentence using examples, explanation, and elaboration. The same is true in an essay. We develop our ideas from our thesis in the body of the essay.

Finally the conclusion of a paragraph ends with a sentence that emphasizes the topic sentence or comments on the topic in some strong way. In an essay, the concluding paragraph does the same job as the concluding sentence of the paragraph.

So, in many ways, what we find in a good paragraph is what we find in a good essay: a topic that is developed and completed.

Look at your paragraph. Now pick out some of the major ideas in it. Make notes on them in the space provided.

Notes

Now work with a partner to discuss what you have done. Talk about how to create an essay from this paragraph. Consider these questions:

1. What else do you need to know if anything?

2. How strong are the ideas you noted? Can they form the basis of their own paragraphs?

3. Do you need to change the topic sentence of the paragraph to create a good thesis statement?

4. How does the final sentence in your paragraph suggest a concluding paragraph?

5. In what ways will the essay you write differ from the paragraph?

Remember that many writers write to understand what they know about a subject. As they write, they ask themselves questions, try to get answers, change their point of view, think of other examples and counterexamples, do more interviews with their subjects, and generally let the writing teach them what path they will take. It should be no different with you. Don't stay with your paragraph just because you wrote it. If your mind is taking you other places, go there. Don't worry!

Exercise 5. Writing on language education   Now organize an essay on language education. You can use the paragraph and essay notes you have already developed or you can write something different. However, if you choose to write about something different, make sure that it's about teaching and learning a language, and make sure that you have a good reason to write about it.

Exercise 6. Peer editing   Before turning in your first draft, take the opportunity to help each other by providing feedback. Take your partner's paper and complete the following outline. If you cannot, discuss the areas of difficulty with your partner. Perhaps the paper is not clearly organized. Perhaps it is not developed enough.

Partner's Name _____

  I. Introductory Paragraph—Thesis Statement _____

    _____

    _____

    Quotation or hook _____

    _____

(Continued)

II. Body Paragraph—Topic Sentence _____

_____

_____

   A. Support: _____

_____

_____

   B. Support: _____

_____

_____

   C. Support: (optional) _____

_____

_____

III. Body Paragraph—Topic Sentence _____

_____

_____

   A. Support: _____

_____

_____

   B. Support: _____

_____

_____

   C. Support: (optional) _____

_____

_____

IV. Body Paragraph—Topic Sentence _____

_____

_____

(Continued)

A. Support: _____

_____

_____

B. Support: _____

_____

_____

C. Support: (optional) _____

_____

_____

V. Conclusion

D Journal Assignment

Write about each of the following:

- Imagine that you are describing your college for your college web site. List ten important features that you would like the world to know about your college.

- Choose one of the features of your list of ten and write a paragraph explaining and supporting that point. Your audience will be students who want might want to attend the college.

- Reread the editorial "A Guide to Good Teaching." Make a list of ten important guiding principles for an article called "A Guide for Successful Students."

- Develop your list into an article. Keep in mind that the members of your audience are students like you.

- Respond to one or more of the following quotations.

"If you think education is expensive, try ignorance."
—Derek Bok

"The highest result of education is tolerance."
—Helen Keller

"I've never let my school interfere with my education."
—Mark Twain

"Education is a vaccine for violence."
—Edward James Olmos

Work

A Prewriting

Exercise 1. Your ideas about work Fill in the blanks to complete each sentence. Each completed sentence should be about work.

1. People who work with their hands _____.

2. Office work is _____.

3. Being a police officer _____.

4. To become a doctor _____.

5. Farmers have _____.

6. The service industry in my country offers _____

_____.

7. The fact that you have a high school diploma means _____

_____.

8. A doctor, a lawyer, and a stock broker _____.

9. The Internet _____.

10. Computer technology is _____.

Compare your sentences. Check for grammatical accuracy. Notice which sentences are similar and which are different in their meanings, attitude toward the subject, and degree of formality.

Next take turns reading any sentence from your list. After you have read, wait for your group mates to read their completed sentences with the same subject.

Exercise 2. Jobs for the future   Choose a recorder and use a single sheet of paper for the group. In the middle of the paper, write "jobs for the future." Then circle those words. Everyone should say whatever comes to mind when thinking of the phrase "jobs for the future." Record on the paper what people say. Do this for five minutes.

Then call out ideas as your instructor writes "jobs for the future" on the board.

Next, pick out one job from the list on the board. Tell the people in the group why you have chosen the job, what its good or bad points are, and what it takes to get such a job.

Exercise 3. From "Amish Economics"   The Amish are descendants of a religious group that originated in Germany. They live in several rural areas of North America. Their principle occupation is farming. The Amish typically do not use modern equipment in their farming, and generally work together for the success of the whole community. They continue to lead a way of life that is not unlike the life they might have led over a hundred years ago. The following reading is by Gene Logsdon, a man who spent some time in an Amish community. He is not Amish.

From "Amish Economics"
by Gene Logsdon

Amish farmers are still making money in these hard times despite (or rather because of) their supposedly outmoded, horse-farming ways. If they do get into financial jeopardy, it is most often from listening to the promises of modern agribusiness instead of traditional wisdom. The Amish continue to farm profitably not only with an innocent disregard for get-big-or-get-out modern technology, but without participating in direct government subsidies other than those built into market prices, which they can't avoid.

Barn Raising In A Single Day

I first learned about the startlingly effective economy of the Amish life when I was invited to a barn raising near Wooster, Ohio. A tornado had leveled four barns and acres of prime Amish timber. In just three weeks, the downed trees were sawed into girders, posts and beams and the four barns rebuilt and filled with livestock donated by neighbors to replace those killed by the storm. Three weeks! Nor were the barns the usual modern, one-story metal boxes hung on poles. They were huge buildings, three and four stories high, post-and-beam framed, and held together with hand-hewn mortises and tenons. I watched the raising of the last barn in open-mouthed awe. Some 400 Amish men and boys, acting and reacting like a hive of bees in absolute harmony of cooperation, started at sunrise with only a foundation and floor and by noon had the huge edifice far enough along that you could put hay in it.

Write down new vocabulary words in the space provided on page 85. Group the words by related categories.

New vocabulary

Pretend that your instructor is an Amish farmer. Write five questions about his work and about barn raising.

1. _____

2. _____

3. _____

4. _____

5. _____

Write down his answer(s).

6. _____

7. _____

8. _____

9. _____

10. _____

Exercise 4. Modern society or traditional society   Reread the story of the Amish barn raising. What in the story tells you that the Amish are a traditional people, removed from modern society?

Notes

_____

_____

_____

_____

_____

_____

_____

_____

_____

_____

Now think about modern agriculture. From what you know about modern agriculture, how is it different from the way the Amish farm?

Notes

_____

_____

_____

_____

_____

_____

_____

_____

_____

Writing to Learn: *The Essay*

Look at these words and phrases. Put them into either the modern or traditional category. Use a dictionary if necessary.

horses pulling a plow   metal buildings
tractors   hoeing a garden plot of vegetables
organic farming   using a rototiller
milking machines   using manure for fertilizer
milkmaid   buying chemical fertilizer
milking stool   chicken coops with thousands of birds
chickens running free   growth hormones
harvester   clover and hay
wooden barns   sowing seeds
family farms   spraying crops
agribusiness

Modern farming	Traditional farming

Exercise 5. Contrasting work in the past and work in the present Think about the following kinds of work. Then decide how the work was done in the past and how it is done in the present.

List and discuss the differences in how the work *was* done and how it *is* done.

Work	How it was done	How it is done
accounting and bookkeeping		
building homes		
communicating		
doing business internationally		
entertaining people		
farming		
heating homes		
manufacturing clothing		
teaching		
transporting people		

Consider these questions:

1. Was/Is the work usually done alone or by a group?

2. Did/does the work cost a lot?

3. Was/Is it something done often?

4. What was/is the role of technology?

 B # S t r u c t u r e

 Exercise 1. Writing a paragraph using contrasting time   Choose one of the types of work in Exercise 5 on page 88. Think of any other differences between how that work was done then and how it is done now. Then write a paragraph using past and present tenses. The paragraph should focus on the changes. Think of possible titles for the paragraph that express the idea of change in some way. Use the idea from your title as the topic sentence of your paragraph. Then continue to write, noting the contrasts in the way the work is done between the past and the present.

_____

_____

_____

_____

_____

_____

_____

Exercise 2. From "Whistling while we work"   This excerpt is from an editorial in *U.S. News & World Report* by Mortimer B. Zuckerman. In it, Zuckerman discusses the changes in work hours now that we have entered the twenty-first century.

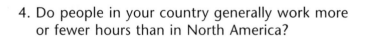

Prereading questions:

1. How many hours a week do you work?

   _____

2. How many hours make up the average workweek?

   _____

3. Which country in the world do you think has the longest workweek?

   _____

4. Do people in your country generally work more or fewer hours than in North America?

   _____

Writing to Learn: *The Essay*

From "Whistling while we work"
by Mortimer B. Zuckerman

There was no big bang as we crossed the threshold of the 21st century, but in one respect we seem to have entered a time machine. "Progress" used to be measured by a more or less continuous fall in the number of hours we had to work—from the minimum 60-hour week decades ago to the classic 40-hour week. But now, in the new millennium, the clock has been put back. We're working longer and longer hours—208 more hours a year than two decades ago. Between 1977 and 1997, the average work-week among salaried Americans working 20 hours or more went from 43 to 47 hours—and the trend is continuing. The number of workers putting in 50 or more hours a week jumped from 24 to 37 percent. We work more hours than any other country in the advanced industrialized world, passing even the fabled Japan. We work the equivalent of an amazing eight weeks a year longer than the average West European. Nor is this a case of the downtrodden masses. It's the bosses, the managers, and the professionals who are working more—wired into perpetual motion by the pager, cell phone, and laptop. And no one—if we are to believe the polls—seems to be griping. Today, over 80 percent of people at work say they are satisfied with their jobs. Noel Coward's aphorism seems to have come true: "Work is much more fun than fun."

The change in the nature of work has much to do with the fun. In 1900, over 70 percent of us sweat it out on farms and in the tedium of domestic service; today only 2 percent do such work. Only 15 percent of us are in blue-collar industrial jobs, down from 30 percent.

Vocabulary

1. Write all of the verbs used to describe the statistical changes:

2. What words are used to describe the opposite of the "the bosses, the managers, and the professionals"?

3. What technological devices wire people "into perpetual motion"?

4. What word in the paragraph means "complain"?

5. Do you agree with Coward's *aphorism*?

Notice that Zuckerman moves between discussing the past and the present. Underline all of the verbs in the passage. Rewrite all of the verbs in the chart below

Past (simple past, past continuous, past perfect)	**Present** (simple present, present continuous, present perfect)

Exercise 3. Shifting back in time   Read the passage below. Then rewrite it in the past.

Our Family Business

Our family runs a small hotel in the countryside. My mother keeps the books and my father does the maintenance and takes care of the grounds. My sister and I have been cleaning the guests rooms since she was six years old and I was eight. Fortunately, it's a small hotel—there are only five rooms. We serve breakfast from 6 A.M. to 9 A.M. My mother waits on tables while my father cooks in the kitchen. My sister and I don't have to work in the morning because we go to school. When we get home after school, we do our homework and then help Dad prepare dinner for the guests. It's the same routine every day except for two weeks in early September and two weeks in early May. Then our hotel is closed and our family goes on vacation.

Our Family Business

_____

_____

_____

_____

_____

_____

_____

_____

_____

_____

_____

_____

_____

_____

_____

_____

_____

_____

_____

Exercise 4. The job interview—verb tenses in questions   Write a list of questions that you might ask a person who wants a managerial position at a very large modern hotel—one of a chain of hotels. Write the questions to find out how much this prospective employee knows about hotel work. Below are some categories to help you organize your questions.

training

1. _____

2. _____

experience

3. _____

4. _____

5. _____

personal strengths

6. _____

7. _____

area of expertise

8. _____

9. _____

knowledge of your hotel chain

10. _____

Now take one of two roles: the hotel manager who is interviewing a prospective employee or the prospective employee.

If you are the manager, ask any other question that comes to your mind in addition to the preceding questions. Take notes about what the person interviewed says to you. On the basis of your notes and the interview, make a recommendation for employment. Should the hotel chain hire the person or not? Explain why.

If you are the prospective employee, use the paragraph in Exercise 3 on page 93 as part of your own personal work history. In the interview, try hard to connect your past experience at your parents' small hotel with the work you would do with this large hotel chain. After you have done the role play once, switch roles and do it again.

Exercise 5. Rewriting interview notes Here is a set of notes from an interview between a hotel manager and a young female graduate of a hotel school who interviewed for an entry-level position with the hotel. Read over the notes and write each pair of notes into a single sentence. Where possible, use *used to* and *would* to express repeated actions in the past. Only *used to* can be used to express continuous actions or situations that no longer exit.

EXAMPLE: worked in a fast-food restaurant in high school / part-time waitress now
She used to work in a fast-food restaurant, but now she works as a waitress.

clean tables and chairs	not responsible for clean-up in present job
parents were in hotel business	no longer own hotel
worked in a small hotel	working for a large, busy restaurant now
learned all facets of hotel business from parents	wants to manage
learned to share work with brother	brother runs a bed and breakfast in town
studied hotel management in college	doesn't have managerial experience
shy and reserved as a young girl	outgoing and personable
parents' hotel only work experience through high school	several different part-time jobs in college
avoided math classes in high school	likes her accounting class
graduated high school cum laude	will graduate university summa cum laude this June

Exercise 6. Using verb tenses correctly—editing Read the following statement of experience and qualifications of an applicant for a position in a college computer lab. Underline all of the verbs. Then find the errors in verb tenses and rewrite the paragraph correctly.

I will like to apply for the position of Computer Lab Tutor. I am feeling very well qualified for this position. Although I never used a computer before I had entered high school, I now competent and confident. In high school, I have learned word processing and working with many different CD Roms. It was also in high school that I falled in love with the INTERNET. At this college I have been taken all of the courses necessary for a certificate in computer technology. I now work on my general education requirements to can get an AS degree.

Compare your paragraph with a partner. Do you have the same corrections? Discuss any differences.

Writing to Learn: *The Essay*

C Writing and Editing

Exercise 1. Brainstorming new jobs We know that new technology makes old jobs obsolete and introduces new jobs. For example, when people in cold climates heated their houses with coal, they needed someone to deliver the coal to their houses. Nowadays, most houses in industrialized countries do not use coal as a heating fuel. Therefore, there are not many jobs for coal delivery persons. On the other hand, people do heat their houses by using solar heat. Someone had to design panels capable of catching and storing the sun's rays to be used to heat some houses. Thus, a new job was created from solar heating technology.

Brainstorm some new jobs. Do not be afraid to use your imagination. You never know what kinds of new jobs there will be. For example, who knew fifty years ago that a person would one day make a living designing games for computers? Fifty years ago, computers themselves filled entire rooms, a far cry from the laptops and palm computers we now use.

After you brainstorm some new jobs, try writing a description of what a person would do in this new job.

Job _____

Description _____

_____

Job _____

Description _____

_____

Job _____

Description _____

_____

Exercise 2. Playing computer games—is it a real job? Read the following excerpt from a newspaper article about Johnathan Wendel, "the first superstar of competitive computer gaming."

"Teen Shaking Up Computer Game World"
by James A. Fussell
Knight Ridder News Service

Cyberstar Johnathan Wendel is virtually unbeatable while playing Quake 3 Arena.

Kansas City, Mo.—Johnathan Wendel is on the verge of realizing many teenagers' wildest dream—making a living playing computer games.

Kid stuff?

Hardly. He's one of the favorites to win a $40,000 first prize in an upcoming computer tournament in Dallas. What's more, game experts say they would not be surprised to see the Lee's Summit teen make more than $100,000 this year as tournaments grow bigger and richer.

Wendel, 19, is one of the best computer game players in the world. And when he plays his game of choice—a first-person action game called Quake 3 Arena—he is unbeatable. Well, virtually.

In the last half-year, Wendel has won Quake tournaments in Missouri, Texas, Kentucky and California. In January he won the world championship in Sweden by going 18-0. In the five months he has been playing in tournaments, he has lost a grand total of three games. He is so good, a computer-mouse manufacturer wants to sponsor him—and put his picture on its products.

Any wonder he practices sometimes 12 to 15 hours a day?

Competitive computer gaming has grown rapidly, thanks to the Internet and the proliferation of home computers. Millions of people worldwide play, and advertisers are taking notice. More and more companies are sponsoring tournaments that offer prize money.

The reason is that hundreds of thousands of gamers follow the competitions over the Internet, ensuring advertisers access to a young, technology-savvy audience with loads of disposable income.

Wendel thinks he can be one of the stars of a professional circuit.

Those who have seen him play believe it.

"I've seen Johnathan in person play on four different occasions," said Robert Krakhoff, the general manager of Razer, a San Francisco company that makes precision products for serious gamers. "And my personal opinion is that he is the top player today."

Make a list of technology-related words from the story about Johnathan Wendel. Add other technology words that you know.

Technology-related words

Exercise 3. Writing questions   Very often when we study reading, there is a list of questions about the reading that the writer of the textbook has prepared. You have just done a reading, but there are no questions. With your group mates, write one question each for classmates in another group to answer.

1. Write your name on a blank piece of paper.

2. Collect the papers from people in your group.

3. Exchange the blank papers with names on with another group.

4. Read the name of the person out loud to your group mates. Then think about a question to write to that person. The question can be a comprehension question about the reading, a vocabulary or grammar question, an opinion question, or an experience question. An example of an experience question for this reading would be *"Have you ever played Quake 3 Arena?"*

5. After you have written a question for each person, give the papers back to the other group.

6. Read each question from the other group to a person in your group. Write answers individually.

7. Exchange papers again.

8. Read the answers to your questions out loud.

9. Discuss the answers.

10. Meet with the two groups together to discuss the questions and answers.

Exercise 4. Designing a job Now that you have read, talked, and written about old and new jobs, it is time for you to design *your* ideal job. Make notes about your ideal job in each category in the chart.

What is the job and why is it worth doing?	What would you do every day with your time?	What would your working environment be like?	What kind of an organization would you work in, if any?	What sort of knowledge do you need for the job and how do you get it?

 Now discuss your notes with a partner. Decide if there is more to add or something to remove from your chart.

Exercise 5. Brainstorming essay titles Here are five different ways to come up with a title for your essay. Try brainstorming as many possibilities as you can for each way. Write possible titles for your essay after each example.

■ Make a title by asking an interesting question.

EXAMPLE: Wouldn't you like to own your own e-business?

_____

■ Make a title by using alliteration (using words with similar sounds in similar word positions).

EXAMPLE: Red Rock Research, Inc.

_____

■ Make a title by giving a choice.

EXAMPLE: Devil's Work or Angel's Work

_____

■ Make a title by giving a job title and a short description.

EXAMPLE: Online Accounting—Where the Money Is

_____

■ Make a title by using adjectives before a noun or noun phrase.

EXAMPLE: A Good Honest Profession

_____

Now try out your titles on your classmates. Consider their opinions. Then write down two or three possible titles for your essay.

1. _____

2. _____

3. _____

Exercise 6. Writing your essay—the introduction   In your introduction, write about how the work of your new job was done in the past and why the way you will do it is better. For example, let's suppose you are opening a real estate firm online. You could talk about how real estate sales were done face to face and how you had to go to the place to really get the sense of how the home or property looked. However, with virtual real estate online, the customer can "walk" into any home or property for sale all over the world.

After you have written about how the work was done and how it will be done, then write your thesis statement, which will link your interests and skills to this new job.

```
_____

_____

_____
_____
_____
_____
_____
```

_____

_____

_____

_____

_____

_____

_____

 After you write your introduction, pass it around your group for comments from your group mates. Then revise it based on their comments.

Exercise 7. Writing your essay—the body   Refer to the chart in Exercise 4 on page 100 to organize paragraphs in the body of your essay. You can write a paragraph for each column of the chart, or you can put two columns together. The choice is yours. You can also add more personal information and make that a separate paragraph. Write on a separate piece of paper.

After you write the body of your essay, pass it around the group for comments from your group mates. Use the following questions to guide your feedback.

1. Does each paragraph of the body have a clear topic sentence?

2. Is each paragraph well developed? Are there enough examples or details to support the topic of the paragraph? Are there any ideas presented in the paragraph that are not related to the main idea?

3. Is anything unclear?

4. Would you like more information?

   Revise your body paragraphs based on the feedback.

Exercise 8. Writing your essay—the conclusion   Write a concluding paragraph that summarizes the main points in your essay: the thesis statement and the topic sentence in each paragraph. Then end with a prediction about how this new job will become part of the world of work in the future. Will there be many people doing it? Will it change even more? Will it become a highly skilled profession? Will it be the kind of work that offers part-time opportunities?

[blank lined writing area]

After you write the conclusion of your essay, pass it around the group for comments from your group mates. Then revise it based on their comments.

D Journal Assignment

You can do these in any order. You can choose to do any one more than once.

- Read the business section of an English-language newspaper. Summarize the important business-related stories in your journal.

- Visit your school employment office or a private employment agency. Walk in and notice what sort of jobs are being offered. Speculate in your journal as to why those jobs are being offered.

- Interview someone you know who loves his or her work. Try to find out why; then write about it in your journal.

- Consider this statement, "Good work honors the spirit as much as it does the mind and body." What does it mean to you?

- Ask one of your instructors to tell you how he or she thinks about his or her classes. How does this instructor prepare courses? Why does this instructor order things a certain way? How does he or she determine student success? Write about this in your journal.

- Talk to classmates who have part-time jobs or who have had them. Ask them about the good and bad points of their work. Write in your journal about what they say.

- Make a work history for someone close to you who has a lot of work experience. Start with this person's first job and end with the present one. Write about the path this person has traveled in the working world.

- Rent *Witness* and watch the entire film. Write your reaction to the film.

Leisure and Recreation

A Prewriting

 Exercise 1. What kind of music do you like? Brainstorm the kinds of music that you listen to by writing down the names of singers, musicians, CDs, and videos.

Brainstorming—Music I like

Now try to classify the music by putting singers, musicians, CDs, and videos together based on similarities.

Classifying—Music I like

How many kinds of music do you like? _____

_____

Now try to define one kind of music by writing a definition of it.

_____ music is _____

_____

_____

_____

Compare your definitions. Notice when someone has defined the same kind of music as you did. Did the person describe it the same as you did? Is there anything about that person's definition that you want to add to your own? Go back and revise your definition.

Exercise 2. "That High, Lonesome Sound"   Read the following passage that defines bluegrass music.

"That High, Lonesome Sound"

"That high, lonesome sound" defines bluegrass music. But what is that sound and what does it represent? To understand the answers to those questions, one needs to understand a little of the history of bluegrass music. Bluegrass music evolved out of the folk music of Appalachia and the blues of the South. The themes in bluegrass music parallel themes in country music and blues: lost love, a cheating heart, a good man gone wrong, longing for the old country home, repentance for sin, and redemption so that the sinner can go to heaven. The individual who is recognized as the father of bluegrass music is the late Bill Monroe. Monroe, who was born in rural Kentucky, played the mandolin, sang high tenor, and led a group of bluegrass musicians, "The Bluegrass Boys," for most of his adult life until his death in 1996, just before his eighty-fifth birthday. His bands set the standard for bluegrass musicianship and ensemble. Many of the current greats of bluegrass, country, and traditional music came out of Monroe's bands.

A bluegrass band is usually composed of five musicians: a mandolin player, a rhythm guitar player, a fiddle player, a banjo player, and a string bass player. Usually the guitarist or the mandolinist sings lead and

---

the other musicians sing harmony. The "high, lonesome sound" of the music comes from the high notes sung by the tenor, often an extension of the lyrics to an intense emotional expression of release or sorrow. It is a sound that echoes throughout Appalachian history, a history filled with poor folk leading hard, even tragic, lives. Bluegrass music continues its popularity into the twenty-first century, adding devotees around the world from Tokyo to Prague.

Write new vocabulary below. Write an original sentence for each demonstrating your understanding of the word.

New vocabulary

From reading the passage, can you write your own definition of bluegrass music?

Bluegrass music _____

_____

_____

Exercise 3. Kinds of leisure activities Decide which activity does not belong with the others. Give a reason for your thinking.

1. a. skateboarding
    b. surfing
    c. sailing
    d. roller skating

2. a. chess
    b. go
    c. checkers
    d. bridge

3. a. baseball
    b. basketball
    c. rugby
    d. field hockey

4. a. reading
    b. gardening
    c. hiking
    d. antique shopping

5. a. movie watching
    b. whale watching
    c. bird watching
    d. people watching

6. a. singing in a choir
    b. playing in a band
    c. deejaying a party
    d. listening to music

7. a. collecting stamps
    b. collecting dolls
    c. collecting comics
    d. collecting coins

8. a. marathon running
    b. weightlifting
    c. iron man competition
    d. triathlon competition

9. a. surfing the Net
    b. emailing friends
    c. online auctions
    d. computer games

10. a. amateur theater
    b. poetry readings
    c. art collecting
    d. book clubs

Create your own lists for your classmates to find which doesn't belong.

11. a. _____
    b. _____
    c. _____
    d. _____

Writing to Learn: *The Essay*

Exercise 4. Classifying activities After discussing which activity in Exercise 3 does not belong, write a sentence that classifies the other activities that *do* belong based on their similarities.

> **EXAMPLE:** *Chess, go, and checkers are all played with moving pieces on a game board.*

1. _____

2. _____

3. _____

4. _____

5. _____

6. _____

7. _____

8. _____

9. _____

10. _____

Exercise 5. Creating a leisure profile Think about the periods in your life—your early childhood before you went to school, your elementary school years, your teenage years, and beyond up to the present time. For each of these four periods of time, ask yourself the following questions, and then write the answers in the place provided on pages 110–111.

1. What was your passion, your strongest interest, at the time?

2. How did you follow your interest? Did you do it actively? Were you a fan?

3. What activities did you participate in that were part of your daily life or routine? For example, were you on a school athletic team or in a youth group?

4. Who were your heroes? Were they heroes to you because they were good at what you were interested in?

5. Have you continued that interest or activity into the present? If so, how has your participation in it changed? For example, you might have once played on a soccer team, but now only play in recreational pick-up soccer games with friends. If you have not continued with your interest, then what made you stop?

My Leisure Profile

Period 1 _____

_____

_____

_____

_____

_____

_____

_____

_____

Period 2 _____

_____

_____

_____

_____

_____

_____

_____

_____

Period 3 _____

_____

_____

_____

_____

_____

_____

_____

_____

_____

Period 4 _____

_____

_____

_____

_____

_____

_____

_____

_____

_____

_____

_____

After you have answered the questions about your leisure profile, then talk to your partner about it. Try to use your answers as a guide; try not to read them. Remember to speak to a person. Look up when you speak. Look down when you read your notes to refresh your memory.

Reviewing Adjective Clauses

In Unit One, you learned about adjective or relative clauses in their full and reduced forms.

EXAMPLES: Many people have climbed Everest, <u>which is the world's</u> <u>highest mountain</u>.
adjective clause

Many people have climbed Everest, <u>the world's highest mountain.</u>
reduced adjective clause or appositive

The reduced adjective clause is possible because the adjective clause uses the relative pronoun *which* plus a form of the verb *be.* Such a reduced adjective clause functions as an *appositive.*

Reduced adjective clauses are also possible and common when the relative pronoun replaces an object in the relative clause.

EXAMPLES: Everest is the name of the mountain <u>that I climbed.</u>
adjective clause

Everest is the name of the mountain <u>I climbed.</u>
reduced adjective clause

Finally, clauses with time, place, and reason can also be commonly reduced.

EXAMPLES: Nepal is a place <u>where there are many high mountains.</u>
adverbial clause

Nepal is <u>where there are many high mountains</u>.
reduced adverbial clause

Adjective clauses can also be divided into

- clauses that give additional information that *is not needed* to understand the noun modified (nonrestrictive) or
- clauses that give information that *is needed* to understand the noun modified (restrictive).

Nonrestrictive relative clause

EXAMPLE: Mt. Everest, <u>which is over 29,000 feet high</u>, is located in Nepal.
nonrestrictive adjective clause

(Continued)

Restrictive relative clause

EXAMPLE: The climbing challenge <u>that is the world's most difficult</u> is K2.
restrictive adjective clause

The relative pronoun *that* often signals the introduction of a restrictive clause, but is never found in a nonrestrictive clause. Notice that the restrictive clause does not use commas to set it apart from the main clause, but the nonrestrictive clause does. In speaking, a restrictive clause is spoken without a pause to set it off. Finally, a proper noun rarely is followed by a restrictive clause.

Exercise 1. Reviewing adjective clauses Now read this excerpt from "Conquering Everest" by Ed Douglas. Underline the five relative clauses and circle the relative pronouns.

"Conquering Everest"
by Ed Douglas

Climbing Mount Everest will never be routine. Despite huge improvements in equipment and clothing in the last 20 years and the scores of climbers who make it to the summit each season, the highest mountain on earth should never be taken for granted. At the summit there is only a third of the air found at sea level and violent storms can rake its upper slopes, trapping climbers in the 'death zone' above 26,000 ft. where the body is literally starving for oxygen. Every ascent has to be planned and trained for in minute detail.

Today it may seem that the route first pioneered by Sir Edmund Hillary

and Tenzing Norgay in 1953 has been tamed. After all, the mountain has been climbed by a 61-year-old man and a 17-year-old boy, by complete novices and even by a one-legged Welsh-born mountaineer named Tom Whitaker. Base camp, 15,000 ft. below the start of the climb in the Khumbu district of Nepal, bristles with satellite dishes. Climbers file daily reports on their progress via the internet. Specialists charge up to $70,000 for a place on one of the commercial expeditions which guide clients to the summit.

The romance and individualism of the early expeditions to Everest in the 1920s, when climbers wore Norfolk tweed jackets and puttees, seem a long way from the confident glitz of this modern era. But one Swedish climber at least has refused to conform, setting an Everest record so exhausting and eccentric that no one is likely to ever repeat it. "Many people believe I am a crazy guy," Göran Kropp says. "They could not be more wrong." The 32-year-old from Yttre Tvärgränd in Stockholm simply believes that if you are going to climb a mountain, then you had better do it properly.

Most climbers who reach the summit of Everest rely on a great deal of help to get there. Sherpas carry their tents and food to camps high on the mountain and use bottled oxygen to supplement what little air there is at such high altitudes. For a purist like Kropp, relying on this kind of support was not an option. "With my project, I wanted to challenge the mountain on its own terms, with no outside assistance." Not only did Kropp plan to climb the mountain alone, without bottled oxygen or help of Sherpas, he also decided he would get himself there under his own steam by cycling all the way from Stockholm to Nepal, carrying all his equipment and food on the back of his bike. It seemed like the height of folly. Those who know Kropp, however, saw it as a typical piece of individual determination, to do things his way or not at all.

Here are several reduced adjective clauses from the reading. Rewrite them as complete adjective clauses by adding the appropriate relative pronoun and the verb in the appropriate tense.

> **EXAMPLE:** At the summit there is only a third of the air found at sea level.
>
> *At the summit there is only a third of the air that is found at sea level.*

1. Today it may seem that the route first pioneered by Sir Edmund Hillary and Tenzing Norgay in 1953 has been tamed.

   _____

   _____

2. After all, the mountain has been climbed by a 61-year-old man and a 17-year-old boy, by complete novices and even by a one-legged Welsh-born mountaineer named Tom Whitaker.

   _____

   _____

3. Base camp, 15,000 ft. below the start of the climb in the Khumbu district of Nepal, bristles with satellite dishes.

   _____

   _____

Exercise 2. Editing adjective clauses—restrictive versus nonrestrictive

Read the following sentences. Each sentence has at least one adjective clause. Identify the clause by underlining it. Then decide whether the clause is restrictive or nonrestrictive. If it is nonrestrictive, put commas around the clause.

> **EXAMPLE:** His commando training which was with the Swedish Army made him physically fit.
>
> His commando training, <u>which was with the Swedish Army,</u> made him physically fit.

1. Everest base camp which is at 15,000 feet is full of satellite dishes.

2. Most climbers who reach the top of Everest rely on a great deal of help from others.

3. Bottled oxygen on which most climbers depend at high altitudes is not used by pure climbers.

4. Pure climbers are climbers who use little or no technology and do not rely on help to accomplish their climb of Everest.

5. Göran Kropp cycled from Stockholm to Nepal where he planned to climb Everest without oxygen or the help of native Sherpa guides.

6. Despite climbing through a terrible storm, Kropp took the time to draw detailed diagrams that showed where everyone was on the mountain.

7. Göran's father took him climbing in the Italian Alps at an age when most children are not yet walking.

8. The reason why Göran Kropp left the Swedish Army is that he was too much of an individualist to take orders even though he loved the rugged army life.

9. Kropp's philosophy which reflects his individualism is to figure out things for himself and then proceed step by step.

10. Kropp is one of the few who have conquered Everest on his own.

Exercise 3. Identifying sentence fragments Read through the passage on page 117, which is a continuation of Douglas's interview. Identify the sentence fragments by underlining them.

Sentence Fragments

A sentence fragment is an incomplete sentence.

- Fragments lack either a subject, a full predicate, or an independent clause.

  EXAMPLES: *Does it on his own*—lacks a subject

  Göran Kropp, a Swedish climber—lacks a predicate

  I like—lacks an object

- Fragments can be dependent clauses that are not attached to independent clauses.

  EXAMPLE: *Although he had climbed other challenging peaks.*

Everything he did in the next five years. Was a step toward his final goal. "It is important to me to stress this step-by-step philosophy," he says. I believe. It is a relevant strategy for all kinds of activity where change is needed. Every successfully completed step enhances competence, thereby increasing the chances of reaching the target."

Kropp has. Climbed some of the toughest mountains in the world. Each a little higher than the last, culminating in K2, the world's second-highest mountain in Pakistan. Believed by many to be the hardest in the world. The following year he climbed another big mountain close to K2 in Pakistan, called Broad Peak. Starting alone from base camp. It was the perfect preparation for Everest.

Exercise 4. Correcting fragments   On a piece of paper rewrite Exercise 4, connecting the sentence fragments into complex sentences by changing the punctuation and capitalization.

Exercise 5. Identifying run-on sentences and comma splices   Read the explanation of run-on sentences and comma splices below. Then read the continuation of the Douglas article that follows on page 118, and identify the run-on sentences and comma splices by underlining them.

Run-on Sentences and Comma Splices

A run-on sentence occurs when two independent clauses follow one another without punctuation between the two clauses.

EXAMPLE: Göran climbed the mountain he planted a flag on its summit.

Comma splices occur when a comma, instead of a period, is used between independent clauses.

EXAMPLE: Göran climbed the mountain, he planted a flag on its summit.

Run-on sentences and comma splices can be avoided by using punctuation correctly or by adding a coordinator, subordinator, or transition along with the appropriate punctuation.

"He's a very friendly, good-natured guy," says Audrey Salkeld. Salkeld is an Everest historian who met Kropp at base camp after his epic bike ride. "He reminds me of a big, cheerful dog, full of enthusiasm and life, But he's also very meticulous," says Salkeld. Salkeld recalls how, during the terrible storm which swept across the mountain that season, climbers from each expedition would meet every day to help coordinate the rescue of those struggling down the mountain By the time the monsoon ended, 11 climbers had died. "Göran would arrive at the meetings with brilliant diagrams to show the whereabouts of everybody on the mountain," he said He was fully prepared to help in the rescue but he wanted to think everything through for himself he didn't want to rely on what other people were telling him."

Exercise 6. Correcting run-on sentences   Reread the passage in Exercise 5. Then correct the run-on sentences and comma splices by adjusting the punctuation.

C   Writing and Editing

Exercise 1. Formality versus informality   Sort the following words and phrases into two groups based on whether you think they suggest a formal lifestyle or an informal lifestyle. Rewrite them in the chart that follows. Add an example of your own.

cheeseburgers and French fries
a business suit
cut-off shorts
a Hawaiian shirt
a baseball cap on backwards
a tie and pocket handkerchief
a five course dinner
calling people "sir" and "madame"
calling people "you guys"
an invitation in the mail that says RSVP
a phone call to go out for a beer
a beach blanket and a cooler

a tuxedo
linen tablecloth and napkins
high heels and pearls
sandals and a shell necklace
a tattoo
multiple piercings
a trimmed moustache
purple hair
a permanent
a pedicure
a wedding at a luxury hotel
a wedding in the woods

A formal lifestyle	An informal lifestyle

Exercise 2. Adjusting to the L. A. lifestyle Read this excerpt from a German reporter's article about adjustment to life in Los Angeles, California. Notice the differences the reporter sees between his Berlin and L. A. lifestyles.

"40 Steaks in the Freezer and a Clean Car in Every Garage"
by Markus Gunther

After two months in Southern California, I am almost completely assimilated to the L. A. lifestyle: I spend three hours a day in the car, nine hours a day in the office, easily call my boss "Bob" and put my feet on the desk every once in a while.

On the weekends I go jogging in Venice with a Walkman and a football cap. All I am missing to become a real Californian is a shrink and a gun in the glove compartment.

But the more difficult part of becoming a Californian was adapting to the local habits of spending money.

When I first went to do some grocery shopping, I suddenly realized: We aren't in Germany anymore, Toto. American supermarkets are huge; one has twice as many choices. Picking up some yogurt, for example, was much more of a problem than I expected. I had the choice of a *low-fat yogurt,* a *fat-free yogurt,* and a *totally fat-free yogurt*—none of which sounded very appealing. Then there was *non-cholesterol yogurt* and *artificially sweetened yogurt* and yogurt with different combinations of *low, free,* and *non* characteristics, as well as a *super-light yogurt.*

Overwhelmed by these choices, I asked a clerk, "Where do I find a regular yogurt?"

He looked at me oddly, so I explained, "You know as a simple ordinary, normal yogurt with milk, fat, sugar and some fruit in it."

But my explanation only made him look at me more oddly.

"Sorry, we don't have such a yogurt," he said, shaking his head in confusion.

Most of what I have learned about American spending habits I owe to my colleagues.

Reporter K., for example, with whom I have been staying the last two months, has taught me everything about shopping, groceries and keeping up the indispensable provisions of a California household.

He has one of these huge refrigerators—twice the size of ours—and a freezer of equal girth. He shops but once a week (whereas we go almost daily) and buys in volume as if he were preparing for the Big One.

K. fulfills some classic European stereotypes of America. The freezer is always stuffed with meat, particularly steaks, and the refrigerator is full of Coke and 20 different steak sauces. About 40 steaks is the standard provision. Whenever supplies would threaten to fall under 25, K. nervously said, "Hey, Markus! We are short of steaks."

What are the differences between the reporter's lifestyle and the one that he is learning to lead in Los Angeles? Use the chart to organize your notes on the differences in lifestyles.

Reporter's lifestyle	L. A. lifestyle

Exercise 3. Lifestyle differences Think about the following areas of everyday life. Is the lifestyle in your country and in North America similar or different from each area? Make notes.

	My country	**North America**
food shopping		
eating habits		
manners		
clothing		
workday		
leisure activities		
greetings and leavetakings		
concern for physical appearance		
attitude toward money		
pets		
car and transportation		
grooming		
other		
other		

Now discuss the similarities and differences that you notice between your native country lifestyle and the North American lifestyle.

Writing to Learn: *The Essay*

Exercise 4. Comparing and contrasting lifestyles   In writing an essay that compares (discusses similarities) and contrasts (discusses differences) between your native culture and North American culture, there are two common ways to structure the essay. They are compared in the following chart.

Model 1	Model 2
INTRODUCTION	INTRODUCTION
BODY PARAGRAPH(S)—comparing all that is similar	BODY PARAGRAPH(S)—comparing and contrasting in one area
BODY PARAGRAPH(S)—contrasting all that is different	BODY PARAGRAPH(S)—comparing and contrasting in a second area, third area . . .
CONCLUSION—summarizing the similarities and differences	CONCLUSION—summarizing similarities and differences by area

Look at the notes you made in Exercise 3 on page 122. Decide on a model for an essay that compares and contrasts the lifestyle in your culture and the lifestyle in North America.

Make notes of your main ideas and organization in the space provided.

Essay Structure
Title: Tone:
INTRODUCTION Thesis:
BODY PARAGRAPH Main idea:
BODY PARAGRAPH Main idea:
BODY PARAGRAPH Main idea:
CONCLUSION

Before writing a draft of your essay, explain your main ideas and how you are going to structure the essay. Be sure to make your thesis statement clear. Then write your first draft of the essay on a separate sheet of paper.

Exercise 5. Reading aloud for corrections   Read your essay out loud. Make sure that your voice conveys the meaning you wish to get across. If something is funny, put humor in your voice. If it is serious, then be serious. Remember to pause and to read your essay by "chunking" the words. This means reading them in groups of words that naturally go together. Here's an example of chunking.

> And one does not simply drive the car in and out of the car wash, / but rather takes a cup of coffee / and walks along the windows, / making sure the car is doing all right.

Remember to hold your listener's attention by making eye contact. To do that, look down but speak up. That means look down to fix the words in your mind, but as you begin to read them, look at your partner. If you only look at your paper, your partner will look at it, too. However, your partner can't read it upside down and far away. But your partner can hear you if you speak up!

Read the essay once at a little less than normal speed. Ask your partner to restate, in his or her own words, your thesis and main ideas.

Read the essay a second time. This time as you read, stop when you are unsure about a word, a grammar point, punctuation, spelling, or clarity in your paper. Ask your partner's opinion.

Make changes before handing in your essay to your instructor.

Exercise 6. My best sentence   Choose one sentence in your essay that you think is a good clear English sentence that also expresses your ideas well. Write that sentence on a slip of paper. Do not write your name on it. Choose one person in the group to read each sentence. Then the group decides the following:

1. Is the sentence a good English sentence? (with no errors of any kind)

2. Does it express an idea well?

D Journal Assignment

You can write about these in any order. You can write about one more than once.

■ Reread the description of bluegrass music in Exercise 2 on page 106. Write a description of the kind of music you like. Bring a sample of music to illustrate your description for your teacher or class.

■ Write about a concert that you enjoyed.

■ Write about a famous singer or musician in your country.

■ Write about folk music or folk art in your country.

■ Write about someone who accomplished a difficult physical feat.

■ Write about someone you know who is obsessed with his or her hobby.

■ Write about a time you went out dancing.

■ Write about a lifestyle change that you made recently.

■ Write about a perfect evening at home relaxing.

■ Write a response to one of the following quotations:

"Music is a moral law. It gives soul to the universe, wings to the mind, flight to the imagination, and charm and gaiety to life and to everything."
—Plato

"To travel is to take a journey into yourself."
—Dena Kaye

The Natural World

A Prewriting

Exercise 1. Things change Think about your hometown over the course of a year. How does the natural environment change? Does it go from budding trees, blossoming flowers, and newborn animal life to leaves, flowers, and adult or maturing animals? Does the weather go from breezy and warm to still and hot? Does it snow, and then the snow melts? Does it rain, and then get very dry? When do the days grow shorter? longer?

Consider the following:

1. The weather
2. Trees, plants, and flowers
3. Animal and insect life
4. Daylight and darkness
5. Availability of vegetables, fruit, and other food

Make a chart to reflect changes in these areas.

Natural World	Change 1	Change 2	Change 3	Change 4
weather (daily weather and special events like floods, hurricanes, or tornadoes)				
trees, plants, flowers				
animal and insect life				
daylight and darkness				
availability of vegetables, fruit, and meat				
personal childhood memories associated with different seasons				

Notice that there are four sets of changes. This is because in some places there are four distinct seasons of the year. If your hometown does not have four seasons, and thus does not see as much change in the natural world, just ignore the extra columns.

Discuss your chart with someone from a different place. Notice what is similar and what is different about the environment in your hometowns.

Exercise 2. From "Millennial Mayhem" The following excerpt is from an article written just before the dawn of the twenty-first century. It brings together the views of scholars and scientists about the century ahead, which is now our century, the twenty-first century.

"Mother Nature's Revenge"
From "Millennial Mayhem" by Jason McGarvey

We've heard it a million times: the water is running out, the ozone is depleting, the animals are dying, and the rainforests are vanishing. But hey, we recycle. We use non-aerosol hair spray. We build wildlife sanctuaries. Heck, we even have a whole day every April called Earth Day.

But Barbara Anderson . . . doesn't have faith in these quick fixes, or as she calls them, "technofixes." Sure, hair spray can be made ozone safe, but it can't be made without water. And if 16 bottles of hair spray use one gallon of water, then 1 billion bottles of hair spray (not even enough to spritz the entire population of China) would drain 62.5 million gallons of water—the equivalent of a small lake—from the Earth.

The only way to protect the Earth's resources, says Anderson, is through "a shift in paradigm." We need to live what she calls "more sustainable lives."

By sustainable, she means taking from the Earth in response to need rather than greed, and at a rate that allows resources to replenish themselves. She likens sustainable living to the Native American ideology of looking seven generations ahead: "The Native Americans never made any decision without considering the impact on future generations." Today, she says, we are barely concerned about our own children's environment.

Using complete sentences, answer the following questions about the reading.

1. Why does the writer use the words "hey" and "heck" in paragraph 1?

   _____

   _____

2. Why is a quick fix a technofix?

   _____

   _____

3. Define "sustainable lives."

   _____

   _____

4. What is a "shift in paradigm"?

   _____

   _____

5. Why are the Native Americans a positive model to follow if we wish to preserve the Earth?

   _____

   _____

6. What positive actions have we taken to help preserve the Earth? (See paragraph 1.)

   _____

   _____

7. What do you infer about the need to preserve the Earth after reading this passage?

   _____

   _____

8. What do you do in your daily life to preserve the Earth? What do you see people doing around you?

_____

_____

9. Many people believe that meat-based diets are harmful to the Earth because it takes a lot of plant life to sustain the life of one food animal. Such people often think that all human beings should be vegetarians. What do you think?

_____

_____

10. Nuclear power can take the place of fossil fuels. Should all the world be powered by nuclear power or is it too dangerous to continue to use it? Should we outlaw it?

_____

_____

Discuss your answers with your classmates.

Exercise 3. Predicting the future   Brainstorm ten areas of life that might change in the future. Then write a sentence for each topic with your prediction of what that change might be.

EXAMPLE: communications

People will carry portable computers and videophones in their pockets.
They will be able to send email by voice and see the people who call them.

Here is some of the language of prediction to use in your sentences.

might   will   won't have to   probably   be likely to   will be able to   be sure to

1. _____
_____

2. _____
_____

3. _____
_____

4. _____
_____

5. _____
_____

6. _____
_____

7. _____
_____

8. _____
_____

9. _____
_____

10. _____
_____

Each person in the group should read his or her prediction. Then the group should discuss which is the most likely change to occur and why.

Exercise 4. Positives and negatives about the natural world Think about your predictions for the future. Are any of them about the natural world? Are all of them positive? Are some of them negative? Together with your group mates, make a list of both positive and negative predictions for the future of nature.

Positive predictions	Negative predictions

Qualify each positive prediction by describing a negative prediction.

EXAMPLE: More endangered species will be protected, *but many species will have died out.*

Now qualify each negative prediction by describing a positive prediction.

EXAMPLE: Many animal species will have died out, *but the remaining species will be protected by better conservation laws.*

After discussing positive and negative predictions with your group, write five sentences in the space provided, each with a qualifying prediction as in the examples.

1. _____

   _____

2. _____

   _____

3. _____

   _____

4. _____

   _____

5. _____

   _____

 Exercise 5. An imaginary journey—freewriting Your teacher is going to take you on an imaginary journey to a place in nature that you love. Relax, close your eyes, and listen.

Now write as much as you can about your journey on page 134.

B Structure

Exercise 1. Recognizing complex sentences   Refer to Appendix IV on page 158 for a summary of compound and complex sentence structure.

> ■ A *simple sentence* has one *main clause* or *independent clause.*
>
>   **EXAMPLE:** The Earth has seen nearly 500 millennia.
>   <u>independent clause</u>

Write another simple sentence about the Earth.

_____

> ■ A *compound sentence* has two independent clauses joined by a *coordinating conjunction* **(and, but, or, so, yet).**
>
>   **EXAMPLE:** There are bound to be many positive changes in the twenty-first
>   independent clause +
>
>   century, (and) there are likely to be many negative changes.
>   coordinating conjunction + independent clause

Write another compound sentence about the Earth. Underline each independent clause and circle the coordinating conjunction.

_____

_____

> ■ A *complex sentence* has an *independent clause* and one or more *subordinate* or *dependent clauses* introduced by a *subordinator.*
>
>   **EXAMPLE:** Some people are afraid of the new millennium,
>   independent clause +
>
>   (while) other people welcome it.
>   subordinator + dependent clause

Write another complex sentence about the Earth. Underline the independent clause and circle the subordinator.

_____

_____

> ■ A *complex sentence* may also have a *dependent clause* embedded in the *independent clause*. This is the case with relative clauses.
>
> **EXAMPLE:** <u>We had a party to honor the new millennium,</u>
>   independent clause
>
> <u>which began this year.</u>
>   embedded relative clause

Write another complex sentence about the new millennium. Underline the independent clause and double underline the embedded relative clause.

_____

_____

Now read the passage from "Millennial Mayhem" that follows. The first time read to understand. As you read the second time, identify each sentence type. Put **S** in front of each simple sentence. Put **CS** in front of each compound sentence. Put **CX** in front of each complex sentence.

"Attack of the Killer Bugs"

___S___ At University Part in Mueller Lab, through a hallway lined
 1
with locked doors, biohazard stickers, and barrels labeled "Danger:

Infectious Waste" is the office of microbiologist Tom Whittam.

_____ Whittam swivels in his chair, and he points to an old newspaper
 2
clipping on the wall inside his office. _____ It's from the *Philadelphia*
            3
Inquirer, 1976. It reads, "16 Die from Mysterious Disease." _____ That was
                         4
when it all began, Whittam explains. When *they* emerged.

_____ *They* were a new infectious bacteria that microbiologists named
 5
Legionnaires' disease. _____ The bacteria had colonized the air-
            6
conditioning ducts of a hotel in Philadelphia. _____ When the hotel staff
                  7
turned on the air conditioning, they unknowingly sprayed the deadly

bacteria into guests' rooms.

_____ "Up until then, developed countries like the United States
  8
thought that they had conquered infectious diseases, thanks to successful
public health programs," says Whittam. _____ But the discovery of
                                         9
Legionnaires' disease sent biologists scurrying to their labs. _____ Ever
                                                                10
since, other infectious diseases have been discovered, such as Lyme
disease and toxic shock syndrome. _____ And despite doing a lot of
                                   11
research, scientists haven't figured out why these new infectious diseases
are emerging.

Notice that at the end of the first paragraph the writer used a fragment. Usually
fragments are considered incorrect. However, sometimes a writer uses a fragment
for a special effect. Until you have mastered writing in English, you should always
use complete sentences. This writer also begins sentences with *but* and *and*.
Students in college writing are taught to avoid this style. In college writing it is
better to use *but* and *and* as coordinating conjunctions.

Exercise 2. Creating complex sentences Read the two simple sentences on
page 138. Then combine them into a complex sentence with the subordinators
from the following list.

Contrast	Cause and effect	Time	Condition
although	because	before/after	if/only if/even if
even though	now that	as/as soon as	unless/whether or not
though	since	since/until	in case
while		when/whenever/while	
whereas			

EXAMPLE: Developed countries had controlled most infectious diseases. New
disease-causing bacteria were discovered.

Developed countries had controlled most infectious diseases until new
disease-causing bacteria were discovered.

1. Legionnaires' disease was discovered in a hotel. Legionnaires attending a conference got sick.

_____

_____

2. You get Lyme disease. A certain kind of tick bites you.

_____

_____

3. It's easy to get tick bites. You wear a long-sleeve shirt and long pants.

_____

_____

4. No one heard of toxic shock syndrome in the nineteenth century. It is a serious infectious disease now.

_____

_____

5. Scientists don't know why new diseases are emerging. Scientists are doing a lot of research.

_____

_____

6. One hunch is overpopulation. Overpopulation may not be the single cause.

_____

_____

7. Some diseases are treated with antibiotics. These diseases have mutated and become resistant.

_____

_____

8. Bacteria existed for a long time. Humankind existed.

_____

_____

Transitions

Some transitions can join two independent clauses into a sentence with a semicolon and a comma.

EXAMPLE: Living near an active volcano can be dangerous; **however,** it can also be beneficial.

Transitions can relate the ideas in two independent clauses. These transitions can be used in either combining pattern.

Contrast	Cause and effect
however/nevertheless/ nonetheless	therefore/thus

EXAMPLE: Living near an active volcano can be dangerous. **However,** it can also be beneficial.

Living near an active volcano can be dangerous. It can, **however,** also be beneficial.

The following transitions most commonly introduce the second of two related independent clauses.

Addition	Contrast
Also,/In addition, Moreover,/Furthermore, Besides,	On the other hand,

EXAMPLE: Living near an active volcano can be dangerous. **On the other hand,** it can be beneficial.

Exercise 3. Combining sentences with transitions Combine the following sentences with an appropriate transition. Add punctuation when necessary. This information comes from an article called "Living with a Volcano" by Dannie Hidayat.

1. The soil near a volcano is fertile. A lot of volcanic products can be used in everyday life.

_____

_____

2. Gravels and sand found in rivers can be used in building material. The thermal energy from some volcanoes can be used to generate electric power.

_____

_____

3. In summary, volcanoes provide many benefits. If you live too close to a volcano and it erupts, it can be lethal.

_____

_____

4. Mount Merapi in Central Java, Indonesia, is one of the most active volcanoes in the world. It is the most feared volcano in a country that has 129 volcanoes known to be active.

_____

_____

5. Barry Voight, a professor of geosciences, sees "the distinct possibility for catastrophe." He has been studying Merapi since 1988.

_____

_____

6. Earthquake activity around volcanoes has been linked directly to volcanic activity. Seismology is one of the main tools used to study volcanoes around the world.

_____

_____

Exercise 4. Punctuating sentences correctly   You can avoid many errors in writing by punctuating correctly. Appendix VI on pages 162–163 summarizes the useful rules for punctuating compound and complex sentences. Punctuate the following passage.

The Sky is Falling

Last spring—in the wake of not one, but two asteroid movies—a story in *The New York Times* said that an asteroid would hit earth in the year 2028. Then a few days after the story scientists announced that they had miscalculated the asteroid's path and it wouldn't hit us after all Folks wiped their brows let out a collective "whew" and went about their business

But according to Darren Williams '98 PhD Sci, an astronomer and assistant professor of physics at The Behrend College we're not in the clear yet There are still millions if not billions of asteroids barreling through our solar system every year Usually either they're too small to penetrate our atmosphere or else they miss us completely But big asteroids tend to have unstable orbits says Williams The gravitational pulls of the planets are constantly tugging at them One could collide with us at any time

Exercise 5. Varying sentence structure Most good writers instinctively vary their sentence structure when they write. Yet sometimes they will deliberately use one type of sentence to create a certain kind of rhythm in their writing. For example, short, active, declarative, simple sentences provide a punchy, aggressive kind of rhythm. Read this passage.

Carter held the pistol in his right hand. He walked with his back to his enemy. He reached twenty-five paces. He turned to face his foe. He raised the pistol. But he couldn't fire it. Fear ran through his body.

Now consider how different it reads when the sentences are joined.

Carter held the pistol in his right hand and walked with his back to his enemy. He reached twenty-five paces, and then he turned to face his foe. He raised the pistol, but he couldn't fire because fear ran through his body.

What difference did you feel in reading the second version with the joined sentences?

The following passage is written in simple sentences. Vary the sentences to improve it.

> The world is becoming a global village. It is a smaller and smaller place. All of us live in this village. We need to take care of it. We are responsible for our basic resources. We are responsible for clean water, pure air, and other living things. A problem in the Amazon Rain Forest affects us all. We must decide to take responsibility. We must make sure the Rain Forest remains healthy and green. In the same way, a nuclear test in one part of the world affects the quality of the air in another part of the world. The Earth is a single living organism. All of us are its protectors. We need to learn to cooperate with each other. We need to celebrate the natural world. We need to realize something. We are a part of it. We cannot live without it.

_____
_____
_____
_____
_____
_____
_____
_____
_____
_____
_____
_____
_____
_____
_____

Exercise 6. Finding writing with varying styles   Bring to class an example of two pieces of writing on nature that use different writing styles. Look among newspaper articles, essays, literature, technical writing, textbook writing, and commercial writing as a way to start. Look on the Internet. Once you find two pieces that have different styles, try to write a short paragraph about how they are different. In class, show your articles to your group and read your paragraph to your group mates.

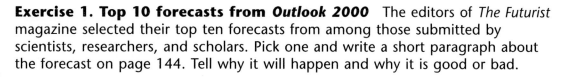 **C   Writing and Editing**

   Exercise 1. Top 10 forecasts from *Outlook 2000*   The editors of *The Futurist* magazine selected their top ten forecasts from among those submitted by scientists, researchers, and scholars. Pick one and write a short paragraph about the forecast on page 144. Tell why it will happen and why it is good or bad.

1. The number of centenarians worldwide will increase from 135,000 today to 2.2 million people by 2050.

2. By 2010, biomonitoring devices that resemble wristwatches will provide wearers with up-to-the-minute data about their health status.

3. Exercise will promote mental well-being as well as a healthier body, helping people fight chronic pain, depression, chemical dependence, and even schizophrenia.

4. Tiny electronic microchips implanted in a person's forearm could transmit messages to a computer that controls the heating and lighting systems of intelligent buildings.

5. The twenty-first century could see widespread infertility and falling birthrates.

6. Farmers will become genetic engineers, growing vaccines as well as food.

7. The worldwide consumption of meat will double by 2050.

8. Ninety percent of the world's 6,000 languages could go extinct by 2100.

9. Water scarcity could threaten 1 billion people by 2025.

10. Human population will level off by 2035, while pet populations will increase dramatically.

Exercise 2. "Ocean Extinction" Read this passage about the extinction of species in the ancient oceans of the Earth. On your second reading, mark the text and make notes on the process that caused the extinction of life in the ancient oceans. At this point, try to understand the passage without defining all of the scientific terms.

"Ocean Extinction"
by Bridget O'Brien

When the continents were moving together to form the giant landmass Pangaea, over 250 million years ago, more than 500 animal families lived in the ocean. There were rugose and tabulate corals, trilobites, bryozoans, and brachiopods, as well as some fish and amphibians. At the end of the Permian period, 95 percent of these marine species were extinct.

"The extinction took millions of years, but had extraordinary consequences for life," explains Roberta Hotinski, a geoscientist. On land, the once-dominant amphibians gave way to reptiles and the age of dinosaurs. At sea, the extinction cleared the way for new corals, fish, and arthropods in the ocean we know today.

What caused such a cataclysm? A handful of theories exist. Some are similar to those suggested for the later extinction of the dinosaurs, including a large meteor hitting the Earth or massive volcanic eruptions. Both events could have released clouds of dust into the air, changing the climate and altering ecological niches. But no evidence exists for either at the end of the Permian period. Instead, this mass extinction seems to have been caused by stagnation, a reduced circulation of ocean waters. "The geological record hasn't shown a definitive answer," explains Hotinski, "but this has become the most popular theory because there is some evidence for it."

Two theories explain how stagnation could have caused extinctions. Either it led to anoxia, a lack of oxygen, or to hypercapnia, the buildup of carbon dioxide. "Bacteria use oxygen to decompose organic matter. As they use it up, anoxia occurs, and carbon dioxide is released. It's the opposite of photosynthesis," says Hotinski. "Anoxia in shallow and deep water is recorded in the geological record. It may have killed the shore life in surface waters. The record also shows that organisms that are more susceptible to carbon dioxide poisoning were preferentially killed, supporting the theory that hypercapnia occurred."

But were they the result of ocean stagnation? To find out, Hotinski used a general circulation model, a computer representation of the ocean to which a scientist can apply wind stress and temperature changes at the surface. The computer model tracks salinity and temperature and then uses physics to describe the ocean circulation. In her model, Hotinski warmed the poles about 12 degrees C as if a warming trend had occurred: the geological record suggests that the Triassic period was warmer than its Permian predecessor. "During the End-Permian period, the climate was not dramatically different from today," explains Hotinski. "The major difference is that the continents were grouped together in one big land mass."

The model showed that when Hotinski warmed the poles, the circulation of waters did indeed slow down and stop. The period of stagnation was brief, only a few hundred years, but the reduced overturning of waters was enough to trigger a greater zone of low oxygen levels in both the intermediate waters (beginning at about 100 meters below the surface) and on the sea floor.

[. . .]

Understanding the Permian extinction, Hotinski says, may shed light on the future. "There are implications for global warming," she says, "but we can't extrapolate too far." The mechanisms for extinction occur over a long time scale, but warming the climate today may gradually alter the chemistry of the ocean. Understanding past extinctions may influence future predictions of how warming will affect the ocean and the atmosphere over time.

1. What is the author's thesis?

_____

_____

2. Where is the thesis stated?

_____

_____

3. What does the author conclude?

_____

_____

Use your notes to retell the story of the process of extinction to your partner.

Exercise 3. Specialized vocabulary   As you begin to read in different subject areas such as natural science, you will find that everyday words are given a specific meaning. For example, in the passage about ocean extinction, the word *niche* is used. In its biological sense, *niche* means the place an organism has in the ecosystem. In its everyday sense, *niche* may mean a hollow area in a wall, an area of a business market that has its own requirements, a job or activity that suits you well, or one that you created for yourself. There are also very specific scientific words in the passage that would not usually be used in everyday speech. An example of this is the word *Permian*. *Permian* describes a period in the history of the Earth.

   Reread the passage in Exercise 2 on pages 145–146 and write down all the scientific words you can find.

Scientific words

Exercise 4. Researching ideas Choose one of the scientific words from the passage that you have recorded in Exercise 3 on page 147. Go to a dictionary and look it up. Then find it in an encyclopedia. Make notes about what you find. Bring the information to class.

  Now use your notes to teach your classmates about the word you looked up.

Exercise 5. Expanding research Now that you know something about the word you have looked up in a dictionary and encyclopedia, you are ready to do some more research. You can use this as a topic. If that does not interest you, you can choose one of the following topics or suggest a topic.

Alternative research topics:

- Global warming (focus on causes or effects)
- Endangered species (select one to research)
- Recycling
- Population
- Organic farming
- Genetic engineering of food

Research tools:

1. THE INTERNET

   Enter the topic as a keyword search on the Internet. Use any search engine. Find at least five articles that discuss the topic. When you find an article, remember to write down the author of the article, the article title, and the URL of the web site. Take notes on what you read.

2. THE COMPUTERIZED LIBRARY

   Enter the topic as a subject in your library's data base. Then read the entries that come up on your screen. Choose five. Write down the information so that you can find the books or journals in the stacks at your library. When you find each article or book, write down the following information: author, title, year, publishing company, place of publication. Take notes on what you read.

3. THE FILE CARD LIBRARY

   Find the drawer of file cards that contains your topic. Then read the entries. Choose five. Write down the information so that you can find the books or journals in the stacks at your library. When you find each article or book, write down the following information: author, title, year, publishing company, place of publication. Take notes on what you read.

Exercise 6. Organizing a scientific essay   Your writing assignment is to create a scientific essay that describes in as much detail as possible the topic that you have researched. Your writing will be guided by the information you have found in the articles you have read. Your writing should also be guided by your audience, your readers. In this case, your audience is your teacher and your classmates. They do not know very much about your topic; therefore, be sure to write clearly and explain everything carefully so that they will understand.

Your essay should have an introduction, body, and conclusion. The body should have at least three major points illustrated by examples. The conclusion should summarize the main ideas of your essay and finish with a strong final sentence.

Exercise 7. Creating a reference page   Follow the examples below in creating a reference page for your research paper. Remember that the author's name is alphabetized by the first letter of the last name. There are different styles for creating a reference page. The one below follows the American Psychological Association (APA) style. It is used for many subjects, especially in the social sciences.

Books:

Brown, A. (1999). The beginning of life. New York: St. John's Press.

Articles in magazines and journals:

Smith, Z. (2000, August 1). The good life. Truth Magazine. pp. 11–15.

World Wide Web:

Fishman, R., & Guppie, G. (1997). Understanding time. Earth Files (online). Available: http://www.geojournal/huh.edu

---

 Exercise 8. Providing feedback on content   Read papers of four different classmates. Attach a note card to the back of each paper with the following information showing how well you understood the paper.

Thesis: _____

Main ideas: _____ ; _____ ; _____ ; _____

Which paragraph(s) was (were) the clearest? _____

Which paragraph(s) was (were) not as clear? _____

D Journal Assignment

You can do these in any order. You might want to do one more than once.

- Write about a famous scientist and what he or she did.

- Interview a science instructor or someone doing scientific research. Find out about his/her work and what he/she is trying to learn. Then write about it.

- Go out into nature and describe what you see, hear, and smell.

- Write about a natural spot you love near your hometown.

- Go to a zoo, a botanical garden, or a park and focus on one animal or plant. Write about it.

- Imagine yourself on a mountaintop in your country. Write about what you see.

- Imagine yourself at the seashore in your country. Write about what you see.

- Watch a documentary of some aspect of nature or science on TV or video, and write a summary of what you saw and your reaction to it.

- Write a response to the following quotation:

  "Only after the last tree has been cut down. Only after the last river has been poisoned. Only after the last fish has been caught. Only then will you find that money cannot be eaten."

  —Cree prophecy

Appendix I
Parts of Speech

- A **noun** is a person, place, or thing. Things can be abstract, nonmaterial. For example, *truth* and *beauty* are nouns.

  EX: that **student, Mr. Smith, you** *(person)*

         New York City, my **room,** the **gym** *(place)*

         a good **book,** our **dog,** his final exam **grade** *(thing)*

- A noun can be a subject or an object. The subject does the action and the object receives the action.

  EX: My **sister** studies **French** in **Canada.**
             subject   object   object of preposition

- A **verb** is an action or a state of being.

  EX: eat, sleep, think *(action)*

         seem, feel, be *(state of being)*

- Some verbs combine with other verbs to create meaning with verb tense. They are **auxiliary verbs.**

  EX: He **is** going to the concert.

         Moira **has** seen that movie.

- A **pronoun** takes the place of a noun.

  EX: My **teacher** is great. **She** is a nice person.
            noun   pronoun

Subject Pronouns		Object Pronouns	
I	we	me	us
you	you	you	you
he/she/it	they	him/her/it	them

Possessive Adjectives		Possessive Pronouns	
my	our	mine	ours
your	your	yours	yours
his/her/its	their	his/hers	theirs

Reflexive Pronouns	
myself	ourselves
yourself	yourselves
himself/herself/itself	themselves

- An **adjective** is a word that describes the quality of something. Adjectives usually come before the noun.

  EX: It was a **beautiful** day.

adjective

- An **adverb** is a word that describes a verb. Adverbs usually come after a verb and often end in *-ly*.

  EX: I did my work **carefully.**

adverb

  He worked **hard.**

adverb

An adverb can also modify an adjective.

  EX: She is **incredibly** interesting.

adverb   adjective

An adverb can also express frequency or time.

  EX: He is never **late.**

adverb

- There are many **prepositions** in English. **Prepositional phrases,** the combination of a preposition and a noun or pronoun, are very common.

  EX: She studies **in** the computer lab.

preposition   noun

Appendix II

The Traditional Twelve Verb Tenses

English has twelve tenses according to many traditional grammar books. They are in chart form below.

Aspect → Time ↓	Simple	Perfect	Progressive (or continuous)	Perfect Progressive
past	John **saw** a good movie.	John **had seen** the movie (before he read the book).	John **was watching** TV (when the doorbell rang).	John **had been watching** TV (when the fire started).
present	John **reads** poetry.	John **has seen** that movie.	John **is watching** TV.	John **has been watching** TV all day long.
future	John **will read** (is going to) the report tomorrow.	John **will have seen** that movie (before it leaves town).	John **will be watching** TV (when I get home).	John **will have been watching** TV for ten hours by midnight.

Common irregular verb forms

Base Form	Irregular Past Form	Irregular Past Participles
be	was, were	been
become	became	become
begin	began	begun
break	broke	broken
bring	brought	brought
build	built	built

(Continued)

Base Form	Irregular Past Form	Irregular Past Participles
buy	bought	bought
catch	caught	caught
choose	chose	chosen
come	came	come
cost	cost	cost
cut	cut	cut
do	did	done
draw	drew	drawn
eat	ate	eaten
fall	fell	fallen
feed	fed	fed
feel	felt	felt
fight	fought	fought
find	found	found
fly	flew	flown
forget	forgot	forgotten
forgive	forgave	forgiven
get	got	gotten
give	gave	given
go	went	gone
grow	grew	grown
have	had	had
hear	heard	heard
hide	hid	hidden
hit	hit	hit

Base Form	Irregular Past Form	Irregular Past Participles
hold	held	held
hurt	hurt	hurt
keep	kept	kept
know	knew	known
lay	laid	laid
lead	led	led
leave	left	left
lend	lent	lent
let	let	let
lose	lost	lost
make	made	made
mean	meant	meant
meet	met	met
pay	paid	paid
put	put	put
quit	quit	quit
read	read	read
ride	rode	ridden
ring	rang	rung
rise	rose	risen
run	ran	run
say	said	said
see	saw	seen
sell	sold	sold
send	sent	sent

(Continued)

Base Form	Irregular Past Form	Irregular Past Participles
set	set	set
shake	shook	shaken
show	showed	shown/showed
sing	sang	sung
sit	sat	sat
sleep	slept	slept
speak	spoke	spoken
spend	spent	spent
stand	stood	stood
steal	stole	stolen
swim	swam	swum
swing	swung	swung
take	took	taken
teach	taught	taught
tell	told	told
think	thought	thought
throw	threw	thrown
understand	understood	understood
wake	woke	woken
wear	wore	worn
win	won	won
write	wrote	written

Writing to Learn: *The Essay*

Appendix III

Verb + Gerund and Verb + Infinitive

Here is a more complete list of verbs that take a gerund, infinitive, or both gerund and infinitive.

Verbs that take gerund -ing	Verbs that take infinitive to	Verbs that take both gerund and infinitive
admit	afford	begin
appreciate	agree	(can/can't) bear
consider	appear	continue
delay	arrange	forget*
deny	ask	hate
discuss	attempt	like
dislike	beg	love
enjoy	care	plan
excuse	choose	prefer
face	come	pretend
feel like	dare	propose
finish	decide	regret
mention	expect	remember*
(do/don't) mind	hope	start
miss	learn	stop*
postpone	manage	try*
practice	mean	
put off	need	
resist	neglect	
risk	offer	
(can/can't) stand	prepare	
suggest	promise	
understand	refuse	
	seem	
	want	
	wish	

*These verbs have a different meaning when used with the infinitive or the gerund.

Appendix IV

Simple Sentences, Compound Sentences, and Complex Sentences

■ A **simple sentence** has one independent clause.

    EX: <u>I visited my mother in New York</u>.
                independent clause

■ **A compound sentence** has two independent clauses joined by a coordinating conjunction.

    EX: <u>I visited my mother in New York,</u>
              independent clause

        but <u>I didn't have time to see my sister in Boston.</u>
    coordinating   independent clause
    conjunction

■ A **complex sentence** has an independent clause and a dependent clause introduced by a subordinator.

    EX: <u>Because I didn't have enough time</u>, <u>I couldn't visit everyone.</u>
           dependent clause   independent clause

Subordinators

Contrast	Cause and effect	Time	Condition
although	because	before/after	if/only if/even if
even though	now that	as/as soon as	unless/whether or not
though	since	since/until	in case
while		when/whenever/while	
whereas			

■ A **complex sentence** may also have a **dependent clause** embedded in the **independent clause**. This is the case with relative clauses.

    EX: <u>We had a party to honor the new millenium,</u>
             independent clause

    <u>which began this year</u>.
    embedded relative clause

Transitions

Some transitions can join two independent clauses into a sentence with a semicolon and a comma.

EX: Living near an active volcano can be dangerous; **however,** it can also be beneficial.

Transitions can relate the ideas in two independent clauses. These transitions can be used in either combining pattern.

Contrast	Cause and effect
however/nevertheless/ nonetheless	therefore/thus

EX: Living near an active volcano can be dangerous. **However,** it can also be beneficial.

Living near an active volcano can be dangerous. It can, **however,** also be beneficial.

The following transitions most commonly introduce the second of two related independent clauses.

Addition	Contrast
Also,/In addition, Moreover,/Furthermore, Besides,	On the other hand,

EX: Living near an active volcano can be dangerous. **On the other hand,** it can be beneficial.

Sentence Combining Chart

	Two independent clauses	Dependent and independent	Two independent clauses	Two independent clauses	Phrase and independent clause
Addition	and			also, moreover, furthermore, in addition, besides,	
Contrast	but yet	although even though though while whereas	however, nevertheless, on the other hand, nonetheless		despite in spite of
Cause and effect	so	because now that since	therefore consequently thus	as a result	because of due to
Time		before/after/ as/as soon as/ since/when/ whenever/ while/until		first, then, next, finally, meanwhile,	
Condition	or	if only if even if unless whether or not in case	otherwise		
Example				for example,	
Emphasis				in fact,	
Clarification				in other words,	

Appendix V

Basic Rules of Capitalization

Capitalize

- The first word in a sentence

    EX: **G**orillas are animals that live in Africa.

- The pronoun *I*, but no other pronoun unless it begins a sentence

    EX: **I** discovered that **I** like to write.

- The first letter of the first word in quoted speech

    EX: She asked, "**W**ho is coming to dinner tonight?"

- The first letter of a noun when it goes with the specific name of a person, place, or thing

    EX: **S**ecretary **S**mith of the **U**nited **N**ations visited the **E**iffel **T**ower yesterday.

- Every word except conjunctions, articles, and short prepositions in the titles of books, movies, plays, magazines, and other written works

    EX: **F**innegan, the **H**ero

- If the conjunction, article, or preposition is the first word of a title, then you must capitalize it.

    EX: **A** Gloomy Afternoon
    In Springtime

- The names of languages, nationalities, countries, cities, towns, and villages

    EX: The **S**panish of **M**exicans from **E**l **S**itio in **Z**acatecas, **M**exico is different from the **S**panish of **S**paniards from **M**adrid, **S**pain.

Appendix VI
Basic Rules of Punctuation

Period

- A period goes at the end of a sentence or after the last letter of an abbreviation. Remember not to use a period after a title.

    EX: I received a letter from Mr. John Jones. It was dated one month ago.

Comma

- Use a comma before conjunctions when they join two independent clauses.

    EX: I tried calling Burt at his office, but nobody answered the phone.

- Use a comma when a dependent clause comes first.

    EX: After Marie filled out the application, she mailed it.

- Use a comma to set off dates, addresses, and titles.

    EX: Dr. John Lincoln, Professor of Modern Music, died at his home in Cleveland, Ohio, on March 23, 1999.

- Use a comma to separate words, phrases, and clauses in a series.

    EX: Dina likes mango, papaya, passion fruit, and guava. Bob complained about the bad weather, his dreary office job, and his boring life.

- Use a comma to separate adjectives that can be expressed with *and*.

    EX: It was an old, dark, frightening room.

- Use a comma after an introductory phrase.

    EX: From the top of the mountain, you can view the entire island.

- Use commas around a nonrestrictive adjective clause.

    EX: Mt. Everest, which is located in Nepal, will always attract adventurers.

- Use a comma with a transition.

    EX: It was challenging; therefore, few succeeded.

    It was challenging. Therefore, few succeeded.

    It was challenging. Few, therefore, succeeded.

Semicolon

- Use a semicolon to separate two independent clauses when they are not joined by a coordinating conjunction or when they are joined by a conjunctive adverb.

    EX: Nuvia loved to work with her hands; she was a marvelous seamstress.

    Il Bum had always wanted to travel to Niagara Falls; however, he had never had the time to make the trip.

Colon

- Use a colon after the greeting in a business letter or a formal letter.

    EX: Dear Dr. Gonzalez:

- Use a colon before a list.

    EX: She had several strengths: integrity, patience, and a sense of humor.

Quotation marks

- Use quotation marks to set off direct speech.

    EX: Ernesto said, "Makiko, you look beautiful today."

Apostrophe

- Use an apostrophe to indicate possession.

    EX: That is Lou's guitar.

- Use an apostrophe to show that a letter or letters is missing from a word.

    EX: He couldn't have been here in '99.

Appendix VII

Titles

Form of titles

- Capitalize the first word.

- Capitalize all words except articles (e.g., **a, an, the**) and prepositions (e.g., **to, from at**). Pronouns are usually capitalized.

- Remember that countries, languages, and people from countries are always capitalized (e.g., **A**merican, **F**rench, **K**orean)

- Do not use a period (**.**) at the end, but you may need a question mark (**?**) or an exclamation mark (**!**).

- Center a title.

Writing good titles

Here are five different ways to come up with a title for your essay.

- Make a title by asking an interesting question.

    EX: *Wouldn't You Like to Own Your Own E-business?*

- Make a title by using alliteration (using words with similar sounds in similar word positions).

    EX: *Red Rock Research, Inc.*

- Make a title by giving a choice.

    EX: *Devil's Work or Angel's Work*

- Make a title by giving a job title and a short description.

    EX: *Online Accounting—Where the Money Is*

- Make a title by using adjectives before a noun or noun phrase.

    EX: *A Good, Honest Profession*

Appendix VIII
Form of Paragraphs and Essays

The basic form of a paragraph or essay follows these rules:

- Indent at the beginning of each paragraph, or leave an extra line between each paragraph.

- Leave a margin on the left and on the right.

- Use 1.5 or 2 line spaces when word processing, or skip a line when writing longhand.

- Use one space after a comma and two spaces after a period when word processing. When writing longhand, be sure to leave space after a period to separate sentences.

- One sentence follows another with no space in between.

Paragraph

A paragraph has a main idea or controlling idea, sentences that support that idea, and a concluding sentence. The main idea appears in the topic sentence.

Essay

Just like a paragraph, an essay has a beginning, a middle, and an end. A typical academic essay follows this form.

Introduction	This paragraph should have a hook, which is a way of getting the reader's attention. The main idea of the essay, often the writer's point of view is expressed in the thesis statement, which often appears at the end of the introduction.
Body	The body paragraphs develop and support the thesis. Each paragraph should have a topic sentence that relates to the thesis. These topic sentences often show the method of organization (one reason, another reason, etc.). The number of body paragraphs varies.
Conclusion	The concluding paragraph summarizes the main ideas with the purpose of proving the thesis or making a suggestion or call for action.

Similarities between a single paragraph and an essay

Paragraph	Essay
■ strong opening hook	■ strong opening hook
■ topic sentence near beginning	■ thesis statement in first paragraph
■ elaboration, example, explanation make up the majority of the writing	■ elaboration, example, explanation make up the majority of the paragraphs—the body
■ concluding sentence makes a strong finish	■ last paragraph, conclusion, summarizes essay and makes a strong finishing statement

Suggestions for writing good introductions—finding a hook

■ use a quotation (the library or Internet are resources)

■ tell a personal anecdote or relate a story

■ refer to statistics (the library or Internet are resources)

■ ask the reader a question

Suggestions for writing good conclusions

■ use a quotation (the library or Internet are resources)

■ refer to the title or thesis

■ ask the reader a question

■ emphasize how the information in the body proves or supports the thesis

■ call the reader to action

Please note that different academic disciplines require different kinds of writing. The five paragraph essay is a good model that will serve students well; however, it is not the only model for good writing.

Appendix IX
Suggestions for Success in College Writing Classes

All of your work should look professional.

1. Buy standard size paper (8 1/2" by 11" with lines) with three holes and keep it in a binder.
2. Every paper must have a heading. Some teachers have a required style.
3. Do not write in the margins on the left and right side of the paper. (Most notebook paper has a red or blue line to show the margin.)
4. Some teachers want you to skip lines or write on every other line.
5. Your teacher will tell you if you should use pencil or pen. If you use pencil, make sure your teacher can see it! Use a computer whenever possible.

Cheating and Plagiarism

Cheating and plagiarism are very serious matters in North American classrooms! Please do not cheat or plagiarize.

Cheating is looking at another student's paper for the answers on a quiz or test, or looking in your book or at papers for answers when you take a test. Copying another student's homework is also cheating.

Plagiarism is copying the words from a book and presenting them as your own words. You need to use quotation marks "..." when you use the words from a book or someone else's words. The North American definition of plagiarism is often difficult for students to understand. Also, you cannot copy another student's essay or paper and put your name on it.

Appendix X

Journal Writing

Journals are notebooks in which writers keep a record of ideas, opinions, and descriptions of daily life. Journals help writers develop their creativity. In writing classes, instructors often ask students to write in journals.

Each writing instructor has different ideas about journal writing. Your instructor will tell you how to keep your journal and will probably collect it at certain times during the semester. Your instructor *may* write reactions to what you write and offer suggestions for vocabulary or improving your grammar. However, the main point of keeping a journal as a language student is to give you a chance to write about your ideas without worrying about a grade or correct grammar. Journal writing is practice in writing and thinking.

Buy a standard size notebook with lined paper. Make this notebook your journal for this writing class only. Write nothing else in it. Do not write other class assignments in your journal. There are many rewards from keeping a journal, in addition to the informal conversation that takes place in it between you and yourself, and you and your instructor: when you have finished the course, you will have a record of what you read, what you experienced, and what you thought about during that time.

Topics for journal writing appear at the end of each unit in this book.

Glossary

adjective clause   An adjective clause describes a noun. An adjective clause follows the noun and begins with the relative pronouns *who, which, that, whose, when, where,* or *why.* An adjective clause can also be called a relative clause.

appositive   An appositive is a noun or noun phrase that adds identifying information to a preceding noun.

> **EXAMPLE:** *My last essay, which was my favorite, was published in the school newspaper.*

base form   The base form is also called the simple form. It is the infinitive without *to.* It is the form you would find in a dictionary.

> **EXAMPLE:** *go*

brainstorming   This means getting all of your ideas on paper or on the board without organizing or evaluating them.

comma splice   Comma splices occur when a comma, instead of a period, is used between independent clauses.

> **EXAMPLE:** *I visited the library, I completed my assignment there.*

coordinating conjunctions *(and, but, or, so, yet)*   These are words that join independent clauses. Conjunctions typically join sentences that are equal in importance. Use a comma before a coordinating conjunction.

> **EXAMPLE:** *I have read the book, but I haven't seen the movie.*

dependent clause   This is a group of words that includes a subject and a verb, but does not make a complete sentence by itself. A dependent clause begins with a subordinator. It must be combined with an independent clause in written English.

> **EXAMPLE:** ***When I was a child,*** *I loved to read.*

edit   To edit is to find and correct mistakes to improve your writing.

essay   An essay is a short piece of writing, very often consisting of at least five paragraphs. Essays typically include an introduction of one paragraph, a body of three or more paragraphs, and a conclusion of one paragraph. In academic essays, importance is placed on expressing a point of view using examples and logic. Students in North American colleges and universities are frequently required to write essays.

focus   The focus is the main idea of a paragraph.

fragment   A fragment is an incomplete sentence, often a dependent clause.

> **EXAMPLE:** *When I read his essay.*

freewriting   This is writing that is designed to improve fluency and spontaneity. The main idea is to write as much as possible without correcting or editing. Freewriting is also called a quick-write or quickwriting.

independent clause   This clause is made up of a group of words that include a subject and verb. An independent clause is a complete sentence by itself. It can be connected to a dependent clause, or it can be connected to another independent clause.

> **EXAMPLES:** *I love to read. When I was a child,* ***I loved to read. I love to read,*** *and* ***I enjoy writing.***

nonrestrictive clause   A nonrestrictive adjective clause gives additional information that is not needed to understand the noun modified.

>   EXAMPLE: *The earth, **which is constantly changing**, is our home.*
>   nonrestrictive adjective clause

noun clause   A noun clause is a clause that acts grammatically as a noun. A noun clause often begins with *that, which(ever), who(ever), whom(ever), whose, when(ever), where(ever), why, how(ever), what(ever), whether,* and *if.*

>   EXAMPLE: *I know **what a fine person he is.***
>   noun clause

peer editing   Peer editing is helping a classmate or friend to improve her or his writing. A peer is your equal; in this case, a classmate.

phrase   A phrase is a group of words without a verb.

>   EXAMPLE: *I accompanied **him to the classroom.***
>   phrase

preposition   These are small words that show location, direction and time, and combine with nouns as their objects.

>   EXAMPLES: *to the store, in the classroom, at the movies, on the desk, from Vancouver, over there.*

prepositional phrase   A prepositional phrase is a group of words beginning with a preposition followed by a noun phrase.

>   EXAMPLES: ***in** high school, **to** the store.*

A prepositional phrase consists of a preposition and noun or adjective and noun. There is no verb in a phrase.

question words   *who(m), what, when, where, which, why, how, how long* are question words. They are also called information question words because they ask for specific information, not a yes or no answer.

>   EXAMPLE: ***Who** is sitting next to Jean?* Answer: *Marie.*

question word order   Normal question word order is (Question word) + verb + subject *or* (Question word) + auxiliary verb + subject + verb.

>   EXAMPLES: *Where was he? Where did he go?*

quickwriting   Quickwriting, or a quick-write is also called freewriting.

reduced adjective clause   A reduced adjective clause describes a noun. A reduced adjective clause follows the noun. The relative pronoun *the* and the *be* form of the verb are deleted.

>   EXAMPLE: *My friend, **looking around nervously**, began her speech.*
>   reduced adjective clause

relative clause   A relative clause can also be called an adjective clause.

relative pronoun   A relative pronoun *(that, which(ever), who(ever), whom(ever), whose, when(ever), where(ever), why, how(ever), what(ever), whether, if)* introduces an adjective clause or a noun clause.

>   EXAMPLE: *She is a person **who** can help you.*
>   relative pronoun

Writing to Learn: *The Essay*

reported speech   In reported or quoted speech, noun clauses are the objects of verbs of speaking. When the change is made from quoted to indirect speech, it is most common in formal writing to change each tense to its appropriate past tense.

> **EXAMPLE:**   *"What are you doing?" I didn't understand what you were doing.*

restrictive adjective clause   A restrictive adjective clauses gives additional information that is needed to understand the noun modified.

> **EXAMPLE:**   *A student **who attends class regularly** is likely to do well.*
> restrictive adjective clause

revise   To revise is to add ideas or cut ideas from your writing to make it more clear and focused. Revising is usually done before editing for grammar, spelling, and punctuation mistakes.

run-on sentence   Two sentences that are written together without proper punctuation, coordination, or subordination are combined. This is called a run-on sentence.

> **EXAMPLE:**   *Ms. Goodnough was my favorite teacher she always made us laugh.*

statement word order   Normal subject word order is subject + verb (+object) (verb phrase).

> **EXAMPLE:**   *I love English.*

subordinating conjunction   These conjunctions are also called conjunctive adverbs. They include *after, before, when, as soon as, since, while, whenever, because, although, even though,* and *though.* Subordinating conjunctions introduce dependent clauses.

> **EXAMPLE:**   *I loved to read **when I was a child. Because I read so much**, writing is easy for me.*

title   The introductory phrase to a paragraph, essay, story, or book is the title. It is usually not a complete sentence. The title should capture the reader's attention or imagination.

thesis   The thesis is the main idea or point of view of an essay expressed in one or more sentences, usually in the introductory paragraph of an essay or in the first few lines of a paragraph.

topic   The main idea or subject about which one writes is called the topic.

topic sentence   The topic sentence shows the main idea or the point of view of a paragraph. It limits the focus of the paragraph.

transition   A transition is another word for an adverbial conjunction. Some transitions are *however, therefore, nevertheless, nonetheless, moreover, thus, as a result, otherwise,* and *consequently.* Transitions can be used to relate two independent clauses with a period.

> **EXAMPLES:**   *I have worked through this entire text; **therefore**, my writing has improved. My writing has improved a lot. **However**, I know that I have even more to learn.*

Credits

Photographs

Page 2: ©Techno Culture and Urban Life/PhotoDisc; **p. 17:** Carl Rogers; **p. 28:** ©Jose Pelaez/ The Stock Market; **p. 46:** ©PhotoDisc website; **p. 56:** ©Ariel Skelley/The Stock Market; **p. 66:** ©Education 2/PhotoDisc; **p. 82:** ©Meetings and Groups/PhotoDisc; **p. 90:** PhotoDisc website; **p. 104:** ©LWA/The Stock Market; **p. 113:** ©David Keaton/The Stock Market; **p. 126:** The Stock Market

Readings

40 Steaks in the Freezer and a Clean Car in Every Garage, pp. 120–121: Markus Gunther, from *Wesdeutsche Allgemeine Zeitung* in Essen. Reprinted with the permission of the publisher.

A Guide to Teaching, pp. 67–68: *The Channels* (Santa Barbara City College Newspaper Sept. 22, 1999, Vol. 41, No. 3). Reprinted with the permission of the publisher.

Amish Economics, p. 84: Reproduced from *Mindfulness and Meaningful Work: Explorations in Right Livelihood* (1994) by Claude Whitmyer, with permission of Parallax Press, Berkeley, California.

Among Schoolchildren, p. 61 by Tracy Kidder. Copyright 1989 by John Tracy Kidder. Reprinted by permission of Houghton Mifflin Company.

Conquering Everest, pp. 113–114: Ed Douglas, from *Saab Magazine* (Issue 3/1999). Reprinted with the permission of the publisher.

Cooking with Mattie, p. 5: Cara Baker, "Women of Strength and Patience" from *The New York Times* (April 5, 1997). Reprinted with the permission of the publisher.

Hands that Held a Family Together, pp. 46–47: Di Yin Lu, "Women of Strength and Patience" from *The New York Times* (April 5, 1997). Reprinted with the permission of the publisher.

In the Year of the Boar and Jackie Robinson, p. 61: Bette Bao Lord, published by Harper and Row, 1984. Reprinted with the permission of the publisher.

Living in Tongues, p. 11: Luc Sante, from *The New York Times* (May 12, 1996) adapted from "The Factory of Facts" published by Pantheon. Reprinted with the permission of the publisher.

Millennial Mayhem, p. 128: Jason McGarvey, from *The PennStater* (January/February 1999, Vol. 86, No. 3). Reprinted with the permission of the publisher.

Ocean Extinction, p. 145: Bridget O'Brien, from *Research/Pen State* (January 2000, Vol. 21, No. 1). Reprinted with the permission of the publisher.

Salam, Shalom, p. 72: Ilene R. Prusher, from *Teaching Tolerance Magazine* (Number 15, Spring 1999). Reprinted with the permission of the publisher.

Teen Shaking Up Computer Game World, p. 98: James A. Fussell from Knight Rider News Service, *Santa Barbara News Press* (March 27, 2000). Reprinted with the permission of the publisher.

The Borzhomi Nose, pp. 41–42: From *Evil Eye Beagle: Funny Sport Stories* by Harrison Powers. Text copyright 1982 by Watermill Press, and imprint and trademark of Troll Communications, L.L.C. Published by and reprinted with permission of Troll Communications L.L.C.

The High Lonesome Sound, pp. 106–107: Lou Spaventa.

This Is Me, pp. 17–19. From *On Becoming a Person.* Copyright 1961 by Carl R. Rogers. Reprinted by permission of Houghton Mifflin Company.

When You Are Old, p. 35: W. B. Yeats, from *The Yeats Reader,* ed. Richard J. Finneran, published by Scribner, 1997. Reprinted with the permission of the publisher.

Whistling While We Work, p. 91: Mortimer Zuckerman from *U.S. News & World Report* (January 24, 2000). Reprinted with the permission of the publisher.